LETTER FORMS

Letter Forms

Typographic and Scriptorial

TWO ESSAYS ON THEIR CLASSIFICATION,
HISTORY AND BIBLIOGRAPHY

Stanley Morison

Hartley & Marks
PUBLISHERS

The essay 'On the Classification of Typographical Variations' was first published in *Type Specimen Facsimiles* (London, 1963) © Bowes & Bowes, Publishers, Ltd, 1963
The essay 'On some Italian Scripts of the XV and XVI Centuries' was first published in *Calligraphy 1535–1885* (Milan, 1962) © La Bibliofilia, Via Manzoni 14, Milan, 1962
Mrs Beatrice Warde's 'Recollections of Stanley Morison' were first published in *The Sunday Times* (London, 15 October 1967) © Thomson Newspapers, 1967
The special contents of this edition are © John Dreyfus, 1968

Published by
HARTLEY & MARKS PUBLISHERS INC.

P. O. Box 147	3661 West Broadway
Point Roberts, WA	Vancouver, BC
98281	V6R 2B8

Text © 1997 by HARTLEY & MARKS PUBLISHERS INC.
All rights reserved.

LIBRARY OF CONGRESS CATALOGING-IN-PUBLICATION DATA

Morison, Stanley, 1889–1967
    Letter forms, typographic and scriptorial : two essays on their classification, history, and bibliography / Stanley Morison
        p.   cm.
    Originally published: New York : Typophiles, 1968. (Typophile chap book ; no. 45).
    ISBN 0-88179-136-9
    1. Type and type-founding—History. 2. Type and type-founding—Historiography.
    3. Paleography, Italian. I. Title. II. Series: Typophile chap books ; 45.
Z250.A2M6925   1996
686.2'24'09—dc20   96-18636

Design and composition by The Typeworks
Set in FOURNIER

Printed in the U.S.A.

Contents

Introductory Note

BY JOHN DREYFUS

Ever since my first visit to New York, Paul Bennett repeatedly asked me to produce a book for the Typophiles of New York, a group which he told me had long been eager to have one of its publications printed at the University Press in Cambridge. He suggested that many of Stanley Morison's essays were totally unfamiliar to his fellow-Typophiles, because of the unusual conditions under which several of Morison's works were first published. My task was to make a selection, to write an introductory note, to edit the texts and to design the publication.

For many years Brooke Crutchley, the University Printer at Cambridge, was overburdened with work. Later he became deeply involved first in planning and building a new University Printing House, and next with the difficulties of moving into it. Such preoccupations are now behind him, so he has been able to print this book in his admirable new surroundings. One of my pleasantest duties as his typographical adviser has been to work on this new edition of some writings by his former typographical adviser, Stanley Morison.

The reader is now presented in a convenient form with two essays which have previously appeared only once, in considerably larger or bulkier formats, one at a high price and the other in an edition mainly distributed to friends and customers of an Italian bookseller who offered very few copies for sale.

⤙⤚

The first essay was originally written at my request to inaugurate a series of type-specimen facsimiles, which had originally been proposed
in the autumn of 1937. I believe it was Graham Pollard who brought together a few people interested in typefounders' specimens and set them
to work on indexing all that could be found, with the aim of publishing
reproductions of the best of them. Four years later 'A List of Type
Specimens' was published in *The Library* (fourth series, vol. XXII, no. 4,
March 1942, pp. 185–204). It defined a type-specimen as being 'any
piece of printing which contains an indication of the origin of the type
design in which it is printed'.

The proposed publication was to reproduce all pre-1800 type designs of known origin. Although the project could not be realized until
the war was over, the list was printed so that the information would be
available if an opportunity later occurred to resume the scheme. The
note in *The Library* was signed by Harry Carter, Ellic Howe, A.F.
Johnson, Stanley Morison and Graham Pollard.

Shortly after the war, I suggested to the signatories that it might be
possible to go ahead with their scheme. With their encouragement and
assistance, I decided to make a start. My original intention was to publish reproductions of the specimen sheets without any explanatory
text, but at Morison's insistence, I agreed to evolve a method of describing these sheets, and to make brief notes on the types shown. A.F.
Johnson, Harry Carter, Matthew Carter, Mike Parker, Netty Hoeflake
and other experts helped to provide brief notes on the types, and also
on the punch-cutters and typefounders responsible for making them.

Two points must be made clear about Morison's introductory essay
on the history of the practice of classifying typographical variations. It
omits specific reference to the first fifteen specimens since these were
only chosen after the essay was written. Furthermore, it must be read
as a general introduction to the bibliography of type-specimens as
listed in *The Library* in 1942. Morison's essay, which refers generally to
a 'corpus' of type-specimens, provides no stylistic analyses. These can
only be attempted when the 'corpus', of which the fifteen facsimiles
formed the first instalment, is finally completed.

-←- -→-

The second essay matches the firſt by ſtarting with a magiſterial survey of outſtanding contributions to the literature of the subjeɾt. Morison concludes with a lengthy digression on the importance of Luca Horfei. Intereſt in the work of this artiſt had been ſtimulated by Signora Marzoli's discovery of a remarkable manuscript by Horfei in the Vatican Library. Later researches in Rome by James Mosley added considerably to our knowledge of Horfei's work, and also produced evidence for considering Cresci an innovator, among authors of Italian writing books in the sixteenth century, in following explicitly the Trajan model. To help the reader follow the arguments, the text of the second essay has been provided with new illuſtrations, and a few textual changes have been made. A reference will be found to Mr Mosley's admirable paper on 'Trajan Revived' in that non-recurrent periodical *Alphabet*, and I am grateful to Mr Mosley for the loan of some illuſtration material. I am indebted to Mr Nicolas Barker and Mr John Carter for their erudite assiſtance in revising the text of the second essay.

-←- -→-

While this book was going through the press, the deaths occurred of Paul Bennett and of Stanley Morison. Although many fine tributes to both men have already appeared, I decided to reprint here, for the benefit of The Typophiles of New York, some recolleɾtions of Stanley Morison by Beatrice Warde (firſt published in *The Sunday Times* on 15 Oɾtober 1967). I cannot think of any friend who could have written a more evocative or illuminating memoir – not even Paul Bennett. Nor can I think of any better memorial to Paul than the remarkable series of Typophile Chapbooks which he conceived and cajoled into exiſtence. This volume is a poſthumous addition to his series.

Recollections of
Stanley Morison

BY BEATRICE WARDE

As a friend and colleague of Stanley Morison's for 44 years, I had plenty of chances to watch the curiously exhilarating effect of that startling personality upon the people who met him. Whatever their walk of life or degree of intelligence, the reaction was essentially the same: their minds expanded to him as greedily as tired lungs rise to a wind from an April forest whipping into a stuffy room.

My own first sight of him was from the back: of a tall, lean stranger hunched like a raven across D.B. Updike's desk, in that great scholar-printer's office in Boston, Mass. Updike had been retailing a story about a bishop's butler, and the room was ringing with Morison's laughter. Then he swung round for his introduction. I had been curious about that new major star in our typographic firmament. What sort of person would he be, who could both range so widely into historical research, and also have the gumption to make the best fruits of that scholarship available to modern publishers in the form of superb new typefaces?

I had already heard him described as 'Jesuitical looking': I was prepared for the black suit and tie, the 'blue' of the closeshaven jaw. What struck me first was the luminous stare of green eyes, fringed all-round with black lashes and topped by brows that arched and clenched as he talked.

In those days he had a formidably clangorous voice and, even then, a psychically alert ear for what you were starting to say in reply to his instantly friendly challenges. His most offhand conversational cracks could somehow burst asunder the hard crust of accepted notions with which time and custom oxydise our minds. I remember the shock of hearing him dismiss 'Art' as 'the opium of the bourgeoisie.' There, by exception, he was using the word 'art' in its shrunken modern sense of painting for paint's sake. I understood him better after his objection to my modern use of the word 'heretical.' 'Heresy,' he said, 'is using part of the truth at the expense of the whole: that's why it's deadly.'

At the Typographic Library where I was then acting-curator, S.M. eagerly inspected the copybooks of sixteenth century writing-masters, and was glad to see my amateur efforts at chancery cursive. 'But now show me,' he demanded, 'how you'd scribble a note to the plumber. . . . Never thought of that? Hypocrite!' – with the curving grin that instantly took ten years off his apparent age.

It was my first intimation that ordinary handwriting and calligraphy were – on their different levels of formality – both parts of the whole art of mannerly writing.

Typography, the setting-forth of the printed word, from that moment fitted in for me as the mechanized sub-section of the whole art of appropriate and courteous communication through the visible word. For Morison, typography was a pathway to scholarly and constructive achievements in an astounding variety of fields. It does offer a fine training-ground for anyone gifted with the power to distinguish between things that differ.

Morison was the most formidable defender of the printed book against obstreperous attempts to 'contemporise' its appearance. But in the opposite hemisphere of typographic practice, where display must shout for attention, that same man devised the famous yellow dust-jackets for Gollancz – triumphs of brash innovation. He once said to me: 'What they call Originality is achieved by getting down to the root-principle underlying the practice. From that origin you think your way back to the surface, where you may find you're breaking untrodden ground.' Those all-type Gollancz jackets originated from the

principle that people who want to know about a book are in the mood
to read print rather than to look at a picture.

⃗←⃗ ⃗→⃗

No one will ever be able to number Morison's benefactions, rescues,
anonymous good deeds. He was secretive about them, on the Gospel
principle that when the world praises your charity you have 'had' your
reward, with nothing left for God alone to notice and approve. But
S.M.'s long months of peaceful dying focused on him innumerable
beams of personal gratitude, for what had amounted to life-saving
deeds and illuminations. He set us on our feet. We shall stand firmer for
having known him.

Typographic

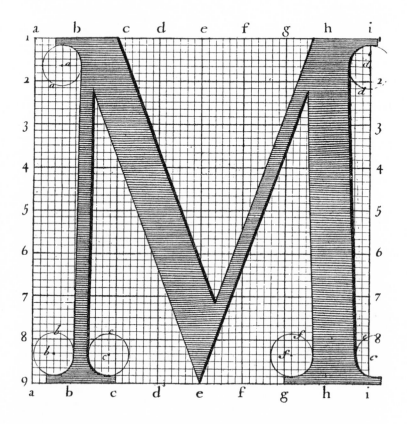

Design for 'The Paris Scientific Type, 1702' (see p. 28) engraved by
Louis Simmonneau for the committee of the Académie des Sciences
appointed in 1692

On the Classification of
Typographical Variations

Critical bibliography is the science that identifies, separates and clas-
sifies details of the physical conſtruction of surfaces and single sheets,
tablets, books, and all other materials to which signs, alphabetical and
otherwise, are applied. Consequently, it discovers the principles that
underlie diſtinctions in the form and the production of textual composition, whether manuscript or printed. The science may, in certain cir-
cumſtances, contribute to the eſtablishment of the original text; the
identification of a subsequent altered version; or otherwise add to the
accurate knowledge of the transmission and significance of accredited
artiſtic and literary remains. Bibliography, therefore, requires an exact
ſtudy of the calligraphical and typographical aspects of the composition, and the creation of a consiſtent terminology for the variations in
letter-forms as they appear in manuscript and print.

The principles of description of the forms of manuscript lettering
were virtually settled by the Benedictine, Jean Mabillon (1632–1707)
and his successors, Touſtain and Tassin, in the eighteenth century.
While the main grouping of pen-scripts was thus effected in the late
seventeenth and early eighteenth century, the main grouping of caſt-
types was not settled until the mid-nineteenth century and later. Nevertheless, as will be seen in the course of this sketch, criticism of the form
of letters has developed the maſtery of its technique. Those who would
appreciate script and type as the basic medium of permanent record

share, in varying measure, a critical attitude towards the shapes they see on the written or printed page. In the case of books printed in the early period, when the shapes of printed letters inevitably depended upon the contemporary written letters, the connection between the studies of calligraphy and typography is necessarily intimate, with the former taking precedence. However, although palaeographical studies enjoyed for many generations an advantage in exactitude over typographical studies, the situation has since changed. During the last half-century, as will be shown below, the accuracy of the analysis of the letter-forms used in printed books is at least equal, if not superior, to that achieved by palaeographers in respect of manuscript books and charters. Even so, the classification of types cannot, in the mid-twentieth century, be claimed to be as correct and complete as the science of bibliography deserves.

Styles, it is true, have been grouped; their historical calligraphic antecedents have been traced by typographical students and reliable attributions made to the artists who, in some instances, have been proved to be responsible for designs created in metal in the fifteenth, sixteenth and later centuries. The rise of national typographical variations in the eighteenth century has been studied, notably by Updike. His specimens comprise the work (1) of active printers, and (2) of influential typefounders, which together amounts to the most considerable of all the augmentations of strictly typographical material that have been made available during the last half-century. Nevertheless, it may justly be estimated as insufficient to supply the answers to all the questions that may be asked today by those who have digested the work of Updike and those who have written under the inspiration of his two volumes, with their 367 pages, some double leaves, of zincographic specimens.

OBJECT OF THE PRESENT 'CORPUS' OF TYPE SPECIMENS

For an art which is dependent for its superior utility over calligraphy upon its obvious economy, something more than the documentation of the hiſtory of ſtyle needs to be attempted. Updike achieved this to a subſtantial degree. Others have traced the development of the mechanism by which copies are multiplied from the hand-press to the machine-press, and finally to the rotary-presses of the present day. The consequent acceleration of presswork has been noted. Thus, the progressive economic advantage of printing over writing has been emphasized. Yet, in the matter of type-design, little attention has been given to the gradual changes in the form of letters that have resulted in the saving of space and paper, and of time in making up for the press, and in the aſtual work of the machine.

Secondly, in moſt inſtances where type-specimens have been reproduced by Updike or others, the majority are heavily reduced in size, and printed without a scale being shown, or the original dimensions being given.

The present new Corpus of Type Specimens reproduces in facsimile the specimens in the original size. The text that accompanies the Specimens carries farther the analysis of ſtyles and observation of regional variations; records the principal ſteps by which the exiſting method of describing the body sizes and linear designs of caſt types has reached its present precision; and, finally, provides fuller and more complete descriptions than have hitherto been attempted. For the better service of the ſtudent, the reproduſtions are in collotype, a photographic process which is universally regarded as yielding the moſt authentic facsimile of the moſt difficult originals.

Briefly, the Corpus is a carefully representative number of documents seleſted to illuſtrate (1) the moſt influential designs (i.e. those that were copied by successive founders) in the ſtyles that were general in the laſt quarter of the fifteenth century, that is the Gothic and the Roman, to which Italic was added at the beginning of the sixteenth century; (2) the early signs of the modification and ultimate supersession of the late fifteenth-century proportions of humaniſt script as they were carried over into Roman (and Italic) type by the seventeenth-century rationaliſt and economiſt outlook; and (3) the transition of typefounding from an individual artiſtic handicraft to an item of manufaᨧure. It is the part of this Introduᨧion to trace the ſteps by which knowledge of typographical variations, and the reasons for them, and the terminology applied in the paſt and present to them, have been accumulated; and how, ultimately, this knowledge became sufficiently organized to juſtify inclusion within the general science of bibliography.

THE EARLIEST TYPE-SPECIMENS, 1467–1592

The firſt source of this knowledge in regard to the fifteenth century inevitably lies in the evidence deducible from the surviving books (and single sheets) that can be demonſtrated to have been printed direᨧly from the forms for which the maſter printers had caused their craftsmen to engrave the punches, ſtrike the matrices and caſt the types. Separate prints or 'proofs' of types made for the information of other printers do not exiſt. Though there may have been sales of type and exchanges of workmen among individual printers in the firſt decades of the invention, no common market, with a type-foundry to serve it, exiſted. It is more than probable, however, that printers with a desire to advertise their capacity to serve authors issued, even in the early period, sheets exhibiting the letters they had available. This had been the cuſtom among the scribes and ſtationers of the late medieval period. A few such specimen sheets remain in fragmentary condition. The earlieſt publisher's advertisement may be that of Peter Schoeffer of Mainz who printed an announcement, datable as 1467, that exhibits the pointed *textura* he used for his Psalter. The sheet, with the specimen line *Hic eſt littera psalterii*, was doubtless printed by way of advertisement to booksellers and their patrons.

A much fuller and more formal type-specimen, designed by a printer and publisher with some splendor and pride as a broadside sheet for the benefit of authors and booksellers, has survived, in a unique copy at Munich, fortunately in complete ſtate. Erhard Ratdolt printed his broadside at Augsburg in 1486. He exhibits ten sizes of *textura ro-*

tunda, three Latins and one Greek. The title embodied in the colophon is *Indicis charaéterum diversarum manerierum impressioni paratarum. Finis*. The words 'Indicis charaéterum' should be noted. There may well have been other printers at work in the fifteenth century who issued such an 'Index' but only Ratdolt's has come down to us.

From the sixteenth century there is one sheet printed by Johann Petri of Basle. It exhibits a large titling, three sizes of Roman, two sizes of Italic, one of Greek, two of Hebrew and three sizes of Fraktur. The sheet gives no headings; it is signed 'Jo. Petreius' and it is dated 1525. Four years later, Tolomeo Janicolo printed at Vicenza a leaf without title which exhibits the range of experimental phonetic sorts in Italic specially cut for the works of Gian Giorgio Trissino. No doubt this record, one copy of which survives in the British Museum and a second at the Newberry Library, Chicago, was printed for the satisfaétion of the author and his friends.

Plantin's sixteen-page (printed reéto only) *Index sive Specimen Charaéterum* (Antwerp, 1567), showing seven sizes of Hebrew, six of Greek, twelve Romans, ten Italics, three Baſtard Secretaries and three pointed *Texturas*, was doubtless intended not only for authors but their patrons. While his title is reminiscent of the colophon on Ratdolt's Augsburg sheet of 1486, it is the new word, used here as a sub-title, 'Specimen', rather than the older word 'Index' that was deſtined to become conventional until our own day. Plantin provides an excellent example of the self-sufficient house which once contained its own foundry for the caſting of type from matrices ſtruck from punches commissioned by the printer himself. It is also an excellent example of the next and laſt ſtage of a large private foundry. The great Antwerp publisher and printer found it convenient to dispose of his private foundry and employ the outside service of an independent founder, and this became the general rule; although in Germany smaller private foundries were set up in the late seventeenth century and continued to operate for several decades. Even Plantin continued to commission his own punches. His engravers retained specimens of the types whose form they originated. This we already know from the surviving proofs printed and signed by Robert Granjon and Guillaume Le Bé I; and it is certain that research in Rome and Florence will uncover others.

After Plantin abandoned his private foundry, he sold matrices to the Egenolff foundry at Frankfurt, which had attracted the services of his practical founder, Jacob Sabon (?–1580). Having married Egenolff's daughter, he became the director of what he made the biggest house of the kind in northern Europe.

Under Sabon's successor, this commercial foundry produced a broadside addressed to authors and printers, headed *Specimen Characterum seu typorum probatissimorum, incondite quidem, sed secundum suas tamen differentias propositum* (Sheet no. 2). This specimen, set up in the year after Sabon's death, is only known in a unique copy, the print of which was 'Verfertiget durch Conrad Berner Anno 1592'. It may have been anticipated by an earlier sheet or sheets, not yet traced; and even the Berner sheet of 1592 itself became known only in recent years. The word 'Specimen', used as a sub-title by Plantin, was to be henceforth the canonical title for this category of typographical 'literature'.

LATER BASIC TYPOGRAPHICAL DOCUMENTS

By this time, the end, that is, of the sixteenth century, there had accrued four classes of documents which are now discerned to be essential to the study of comparative typography. First, the work of the printer himself, whether of the fifteenth century or later, for example Caxton's production as studied by Blades (see below); secondly, the archive of the printer, for example the correspondence of Johann Amerbach of Basle as edited by Hartmann, and of Plantin as edited by Rooses (see below); thirdly, the 'Specimen' issued by the printer for his own convenience or to attract authors which, later on, in the hand of the independent or commercial founder advertised his types to the printer, author and others. Finally there remain, in the ancient printing houses, punches and matrices, etc., which throw light on methods of cutting and founding.

After Ratdolt's broadside *Index* of 1486, and Plantin's booklet *Index sive Specimen* of 1567, the immediate succession of 'Specimens' was, so to say, indireƈt. The Frankfurt foundry (and its subsidiaries) dominated the trade in the late sixteenth and seventeenth centuries. But the imperial city was not deſtined to hold its primacy.

Georg Leopold Fuhrmann, who printed his *Designatio Typorum et Charaƈterum Officinae Chalcographiae* of 1616, was a printer and bookseller at Nuremberg. Annexed to his bookshop he had not only a composing room and press room, but also a small private foundry. His is the firſt known 'Specimen' made in a maſter's own office since Plantin issued his 'Specimen' in 1567; and the firſt Specimen from a South German office. Like Plantin's *Index*, it is a book, but unlike Plantin's book it is a piece of personal publicity, and as such a much more elaborate produƈtion. Twelve pages of prelims (of no intereſt) are followed by twenty-four pages of 'Fraƈtur' and 'Schwobocher' (*sic*) some of which are worth ſtudying. Under the heading 'Sequuntur typi Latini', Fuhrmann next illuſtrates, in twenty-four pages, six Romans, four Italics and two sizes of Greek. These specimens are all printed reƈto only (in Plantin's ſtyle). The music and calendar signs which occupy twelve pages are moſtly printed reƈto and verso. The concluding fifty-four pages of decorated gothic initials and ornamental ſtrips are printed reƈto and verso. The whole forms a subſtantial book, very remarkable for its year, 1616, and its place, Nuremberg.

An early specimen was printed by Jean or Johann Schmidt of Porrentruy, a town in French-speaking Switzerland situated in the southweſt of the diocese of Basle, whose bishops had a château there which they made their permanent residence in 1527. Schmidt's specimen is a small folio broadside which shows the Luther Romans and Italics classed as 'Garamond'. Its main intereſt is its date, 1600. Schmidt doubtless printed for the bishop of Basle, but his office was in no sense inſtitutional.

The *Indice de Caratteri* of the Stamperia Vaticana, printed in 1628, is the original 'Index' issued from the firſt inſtitutional Press, created by

Sixtus V in 1587. It is also the firSt to exhibit a range of Oriental, in addition to the usual Roman and Italic and founts of Greek, many of which, like the Frankfurt faces, originated with Garamond, Granjon and Le Bé I. The inclusion of exotics is notable. The like was not seen elsewhere for a century.

Meanwhile, as a commercial house, the Egenolff-Sabon-Berner-Luther foundry at Frankfurt continued to issue sheets of Roman and Italic (principally) in succession to the 'Specimen' of 1592. Specimens are known dated 1622, 1664, 1665, 1670 (Greek only), 1678 (Fraktur), 1718 (Roman and Italic). Fievet of Frankfurt issued specimens in Roman and Italic, caSt mainly from the Sabon-Berner-Luther matrices, dated 1664, and 1682 (including Hebrew). Reinhard Voskens of Frankfurt published a specimen of Roman, Italic and Fraktur c. 1670; J.A. Schmidt, also of Frankfurt, published a specimen of Fraktur in 1675, and other Fraktur specimens were issued in Frankfurt by Rolloux (1714) and Stubenvoll (1713 and 1717). Roman and Italics from the old Sabon-Berner-Luther matrices appear in all these specimens. The reason why Fraktur is mentioned here will appear presently. The lead taken by the German foundries using French designs is noteworthy. Doubtless England received supplies of type from both countries. No specimen of type for sale by an English founder is known before Moxon's of 1669 and, since the trade was SriÉtly regulated in the intereSts of a small group of printers and booksellers, it is unlikely that such specimens were required in quantity until the laSt decades of the seventeenth century. London was dependent upon foreign punches and upon foreign punch-cutters.

An important continental specimen is that of the native Transylvanian, Kis Miklòs, *alias* Nicolaus Klein, who laboured in AmSterdam. The researches of Mr Harry Carter and Mr George Buday in 1957 and Mr Tibor Szántó in 1958 have not enabled them to date it precisely, but they adduce faÉts that place it at AmSterdam between 1680 and 1689. The important faÉt is that Kis cut, or procured from the trade, an impressive series of Romans, Italics and exotics. It is hoped that a reproduction direct from the original may be obtained for inclusion in a later fascicule of this Corpus.

ENGLISH AND SCOTTISH SPECIMENS, 1683–1713

In 1683–4, however, England produced the first book of a class for which no continental equivalent had been produced. Joseph Moxon's *Mechanick Exercises* was not indebted to any previous writer. This is a most remarkable achievement. Moxon's is an original work of great value to students of the art of printing in the operative sense. As his title proclaims, the author intends a practical treatise on punch-cutting and letter-founding 'kept so conceal'd among the Artificers of it'. *Proves of Several Sorts of Letters Cast by Joseph Moxon* is the title of the Specimen, showing seven sizes of 'Romain' and four of 'Italic' that he printed, in folio, with the imprint 'Westminster Printed by Joseph Moxon, in Russel Street, at the Signs of the Atlas. 1669.' The evidence available does not demonstrate that Moxon cut the punches; nor does his sheet of *Proves* make the claim.

The work of the independent (that is, those working for several houses) London punch-cutters such as Nicholls (*c.* 1665) and Grover (*c.* 1690) is of interest, as showing the level of craftsmanship in England, whose trade had for so long relied upon imported punches and matrices.

Next, the University of Oxford produced, in 1693, its first *Specimen of the several Sorts of Letter given to the University by John Fell*. All of these, until lately, were believed to be of Dutch design of the seventeenth century but have now been shown to be of the French sixteenth century. In 1709 there appeared in Edinburgh *A Specimen of the Types in John Moncur's Printing House . . . printed by the Owner of the Types*. Moncur's founts were Dutch, like those of James Watson, also of Edinburgh, who published in 1713 an historical and documented 'Specimen', the first of the kind to be published in Britain. The historical material that Watson provided is drawn from Jean de la Caille's

Histoire de l'Imprimerie published in Paris in 1689. Watson also provides a sketch of Scottish typographical history.

More significant than the English or Scottish 'Proves' or 'Specimens' is the first appreciation of the art by a practicing professor or an author, *De Germaniae Miraculo optimo maximo, Typis literarum, earumque differentiis, Dissertatio,* etc. Paul Pater was a professor of mathematics and astronomy at Danzig. He had a precise mind which, while of a scholastic turn, was also practical. His book appeared at Leipzig in 1710. It is historical, descriptive and economic. He possessed, or had seen, a collection of typefounders' Specimens, for he refers (p. 1) to them under the generic title 'Specimen Probatissimorum Typorum'. As he mentions (p. 18) Granion (*sic*) and Garamond, Pater must have known the Berner and Luther sheets of 1592 or 1612. Also, Pater could hardly have failed to collect a copy of Fuhrmann's work printed in Nuremberg in 1616 and to have read his preliminary 'Dissertatiuncula'. But, although writing as an author, Pater was also of a businesslike turn of mind. Among the headings to his paragraphs at p. 86 is 'Quantum lucri ex uno prelo typographico singulis hebdomatibus obvenire possit?'

His third chapter 'De Differentia Typorum, et varia eorum appellatione' is the first attempt to group and classify the types then available, as Pater says, in the best ordered offices in Amsterdam, Leipzig, Nuremberg, Frankfurt and elsewhere. He laments the lack of a typographical nomenclature common to Europe and, in effect, he abandons the task either of standardizing the names, or relating the sizes. Instead he shows the best faces (Roman, Italic, Fraktur, and founts of Greek, Hebrew and some exotics) that he could persuade his excellent printer Johann Friedrich Gleditsch of Leipzig to collect. At pp. 29, 30 he offers some particulars about the founts acquired by Wolfgang Dietrich Ehrhard of Leipzig; a matter to which reference is made later in this Introduction.

Pater's is, typographically, a finely composed work, though printed, like all German books of the period, on a thin, soft, laid paper which ha-

bitually foxes. The *Dissertatio* has all the marks of a book produced at
the expense of an author who knew precisely what he wanted, and how
to get it. On the day of publication it muſt then have looked a wonderful piece to his friends, though its title page is a little too wonderful for
us. The chapter openings are graced with some handsome ornamental
initials, cut on wood according to his specifications (if not designs).

It is refreshing to find Pater praised in *Typographia Jubilans* by
Friedrich Chriſtian Lesser, the scholarly paſtor at Nordhausen, who
thus celebrated the third centenary of the invention, in 1740. Lesser
was an antiquarian, a colleƈtor of engravings, printers' marks and all
kinds of typographical bric-à-brac. Lesser, however, knew little about
the hiſtory of typefounding and says so (p. 133) but he knew Pater's
Dissertatio. 'Das iſt von dem beſten und groeſten Wunder-Werke
Teutschlandes, deren gegossenen Buchſtaben, und deren Under-
schiede in welcher er kurtz, aber gut, die gantze Beschaffenheit der
Buchdruckerei abgehandelt hat' (p. 12). Notwithſtanding, Pater has
since been negleƈted by the typographical scholars of his own nation,
who, apart from Guſtav Mori, have concentrated upon early and modern printing. A reprint of Pater, edited by a German scholar, is very desirable.

Lesser was also acquainted with the work of Johann Heinrich Gott-
fried Erneſti, *Die wol-eingerichtete Buchdruckerey, mit hundert und ein
und ʒwanʒig Teutsch, Lateinisch, Griechisch und Hebräischen Schrifften*
(Nuremberg, 1721; 1733). This oblong oƈtavo is the largeſt and, up
to that time, the beſt documented colleƈtion of Weſtern, Oriental and
Asiatic founts then available in the German trade, as diſtinƈt from the
particular colleƈtions available from individual typefounders. Erneſti's
book surpasses the *Dissertatiuncula* of 1616 of Fuhrmann, rivals the
Vatican *Indice* of 1628, and easily supersedes the *Dissertatio* of 1710 of
Pater, because it ranges far more widely. Erneſti symbolizes moſt
effeƈtively the degree of competition being given by Nuremberg to the
Amſterdam and Frankfurt typefoundries. He is proud of the achievements of Nuremberg and its 'berühmten Schrifftschneidern und

Schrifftgiessern, Georg Albert Baumann, Ulrich Pfeiffern, und Johann Chriſtoph Schützen'. His exotics form a remarkable colleƈtion.

LEIPZIG *v.* FRANKFURT

The rise of Leipzig to a principal position in the German bookselling trade, and the increasing importance of Nuremberg, were two major faƈtors that effeƈted a permanent change, at the expense of Frankfurt, and of the type-designs so long associated with the foundries in the city of Mallinkrodt described in 1640 as 'Francofurtum Europae umbilicus et centrum'.

The domination of the Frankfurt designs, which was based on the superior preſtige of Paris and Antwerp over Basle, and on the renown of Garamond and Granjon, began to be undermined in the seventeenth century. Publishers migrated from Frankfurt to enjoy the greater peace and freedom of the Proteſtant cities such as Nuremberg; and later and more principally Leipzig. The Saxon city's fairs, which flourished notwithſtanding Leipzig's own troubles, were of benefit to the publishing trade. Some account of the rivalry between the old and new centres of publishing is given in the account which James Weſtfall Thompson and Harrison C. Dale published in 1910. It may suffice here to point out that Leipzig's book fair had its firſt printed catalogue in 1595 (Henning Grosse). While Frankfurt's firſt catalogue was printed in 1564 (Georg Willer), it ceased publication in 1592 when Leipzig began to overshadow Frankfurt in output.

In sum, Frankfurt had for two centuries, or more, organized a virtual monopoly for the French Romans and French Italics which they caſt upon German bodies which were too large. By its international marketing methods Frankfurt blocked progress in the rationalization of the Aldine and Garamond-Granjon designs. These had, firſt through Paris, secondly through Antwerp and laſtly through Frankfurt, dominated all European typography in Latin and many of the vernaculars. However, at laſt, the design that had a preſtige undimmed and uninterrupted since 1495 was obliged, say after 1595, to face very severe competition; and by, say, 1695 it was obliged to acknowledge defeat by the Leipzig typefoundries and their designers. The fundamental weakness of the Garamond and Granjon designs as cast in Frankfurt was that the face, in the principal sizes used, had always been too small for its body.

THE PARAMOUNT FRANKFURT ROMAN (GARAMOND) THREATENED BY LEIPZIG

The present Corpus will make possible, for the first time, close comparison of body sizes and will establish the mathematical relation, for example, of the French, German, English and Dutch 'Cicéro'. It was an economic disadvantage to the printer when, as in the instance of such a frequently used body as 'Cicéro', the German body was larger than the French. In other words, while the Paris 'Garamond' filled the body, the same face cast from the same matrices upon the Frankfurt equivalent did not. Space was thereby wasted, which in the case of a long text was a consideration.

It must not be forgotten, also, that the original Garamond was a secondary translation into type, by way of Aldus's original, of a late humanist script. Thus Paris, Antwerp and Frankfurt honoured the old calligraphical proportions, and continued to do so until at least the third quarter of the seventeenth century. Thus, even when 'Garamond' was cast upon a French body, its projectors (b, d, l, g, p, y) were longer than necessary and waste of space was thereby again made inevitable. There is a third point, related to space-saving, to be mentioned later. The matter, as a whole, is one that requires far closer investigation than is possible in the present state of knowledge, which, as has been said, will be largely increased when the present Corpus of facsimiles is complete. All that can be done in this sketch is to refer the reader to two specimens at D2 and D3 of Fuhrmann's Specimen of 1616, each of which exhibits an 'Antiqua quam mediam vocant', but the first of which is designated 'Francofurti fusa' and the second 'Norim-bergae fusa'. The sceptical reader will there perceive the point of the comparison, namely that the Nuremberg casting is new in so far as it gives a larger face on the body. This is the first datable specimen of such a Roman.

This specimen of the Roman 'Norimbergae fusa' implies a direct criticism of the Frankfurt, or 'Garamond', design. No explicit refer-ence is made to it. The Nuremberg casting is the handiwork of a crafts-man by no means expert according to Frankfurt standards; but he seems to have made a second innovation for, according to the specimen shown, his larger face is cast, not upon the equivalent, but upon a smaller body than the normal Frankfurt 'Mittel', which is the equiva-lent of the Paris 'Gros Texte'. It is necessary, at this period, to empha-size the scantiness of our present information in this respect. It is not suggested that the casting of a face originally designed for one body upon a smaller body was first achieved in the sixteenth century; it may well have been done successfully in, say, Venice in the fifteenth century and, later, in Paris. It was certainly achieved in Antwerp by Plantin. His Inventory of 1595 exhibits an 'Augustin sur la Mediane', that is the equivalent of a 12-point Didot on an 11-point Didot body; a Didot point being 0.3759 mm. The mensuration of the German bodies in the sixteenth and seventeenth centuries urgently needs tabulation before reliable statements can be made about developments after Fuhrmann and Jannon.

There had been isolated criticism by punch-cutters, as opposed to founders, of the current designs as far back as the lifetime of the greatest exponent of the Aldine roman tradition Claude Garamond. The first types to depart from the accepted proportions by enlarging the x-height to that normally found in the size above were a set of five Romans from *Texte* to *Garamonde* cut between 1557 and 1559 by Pierre Haultin, a French punch-cutter and contemporary of Garamond's, for Paolo Manuzio of Venice. Granjon cut a similar face by 1568, called *Gros Cicero* in the *c.* 1598 Le Bé II Inventory; Sanleque cut one, found in the same inventory, and so did Jean Jannon of Sedan who showed it in his 1621 *Espreuve des Caractères Nouvellement Taillez*. However, for the moſt part the Aldine tradition as interpreted by Garamond and caſt at Frankfurt persiſted. When the economic rationalization of Romans did take effeƈt it came as the result of pressure upon Frankfurt from outside foundries, principally those of Leipzig.

THE SPREAD OF THE VERNACULAR AND THE TRIUMPH OF LEIPZIG

There were several reasons for the final decline of Frankfurt. Some reasons have already been mentioned. There are others. The book trade of the imperial city had long been international in range. Booksellers from Paris, Antwerp, Venice, Amſterdam, London and elsewhere were regularly at Frankfurt and between 1564 and 1600 the fair catalogues liſt 14,724 publications from German and 6,113 from foreign presses – plus 1,014 without imprint. Later, the representation of non-German presses declined; so, too, did the proportion of books in the language of scholars, Latin. Accordingly, the figures assembled in F. Kapp, *Geschichte des deutschen Buchhandels* (Leipzig, 1886) following G. Schwetschke, *Mess-Jahrbücher des deutschen Buchhandels* (Halle, 1850), for Latin and German books handled at Frankfurt between 1561 and 1565, are 403 and 280 respeƈtively; and in 1661–5 they are 539 and 328 respeƈtively. Twenty-four years later, the figures for Latin and German books were equal. Also, during the same period, according to F. von Schroeder, *Die Verlegung der Büchermesse von Frankfurt a. M. nach Leipzig* (Leipzig, 1904), between 1565 and 1605 the output of Catholic theological books as againſt Proteſtant had ſteadily declined, except between 1629 and 1631 (when there was a temporary Catholic gain). In 1685 there were fifty-four Catholic books as againſt 254 Proteſtant, and of these 109 were printed at Leipzig. It will be borne in mind that Proteſtant edifying literature was predominantly German in language.

From 1680 the number of German books was nearly equal to the
Latin in total. Concurrently, Leipzig rose to a primary position of the
national, rather than international, German book trade. Also, it was
enabled, by the development of its banking and credit system, to extend
business beyond the range of any fair fixed at half-yearly intervals.

The significant typographical concomitant of the steady rise of
composition in German instead of Latin meant a great accession of vi-
tality in the cutting of a letter-form that had first been devised for charters and books in Latin. A variant of this diplomatic form was
established for use in the Imperial Chancery. It was taught publicly by
Johann (the elder) Neudörffer, the writing-master of Nuremberg,
whose first writing manual was the *Fundament* of 1519. His first manual
of writing uses Latin as the medium for what the elder Neudörffer later
(1538) helped to organize as the future national script for the German
language. This kind of lettering is a version of black-letter inflected
with cursive and given the dubious benefit of decorative flourishes that
qualify it for the description of baroque. It cannot be denied that, as it
originally appeared in type in Augsburg in 1513, printed by Schön-
sperger, it looks well. The *Horae* dedicated to Maximilian makes a very
handsome appearance. However, any aesthetic appeal it may have is
not of interest here. What is important is that the first Fraktur type obviously descends from the Gothic 'Textura'. The term 'Fractura' is of
late medieval origin.

THE 'FRAKTUR' AND THE ECONOMIC RATIONALIZATION
OF FACE AND BODY

The interested will find its early history well set forth by Ernst Crous,
'Die gotischen Schriftarten im Buchdruck' in E. Crous and J. Kirchner,
Die gotischen Schriftarten (Leipzig, 1928). 'Fraktur' is a face that made
hardly any impression on the English book trade and has, therefore, no
interest to the modern English reader, or contemporary English typographer. Some apology is due for the inclusion here of what must seem,

at first sight, to be an irrelevance. The fact is, however, that the scientific student of typographical history and practice needs to observe two points about Fraktur: (1) that its later, that is, sixteenth-century versions, cut in any size, fit the respective German body more closely than either Roman or Italic; and (2) that even had Fraktur, like Roman, been cast upon a body slightly larger than necessary, it still had the advantage in size and real legibility. It is necessary to recognize that, especially in sizes below 'tertia' or 'gros Romain', Fraktur is more legible and more economic than its Roman counterparts, and that it does not lose its legibility until it is forced to submit to the decorative tricks of the writing-masters, such as the artificial, instead of functional, breaking of the curves and the addition of over-exuberant decoration. It is not surprising, therefore, that in the last quarter of the seventeenth century, when the German bookselling trade found Leipzig a more convenient centre than Frankfurt, the local punch-cutters assimilated the proportions of Roman and Italic customary in Frankfurt to those of 'Fraktur'.

The advantage that Fraktur enjoys in legibility and economy derives from its medieval pedigree. Black-letter superseded the lighter minuscule standardized by Charlemagne for reasons unconnected with architecture, but closely connected with economy. By a process that occupied more than a century, the Carolingian script reached its maturity at Tours. At St Gall, the best scribes shortened the projectors and thickened the strokes. Next, they reduced the width of the letter. By the beginning of the eleventh century the scribes had created a letter-form that had two distinct economic advantages over the older script. It was these advantages that, when later formalized by professional scribes, produced what is known as 'Textura' – highly condensed in northern Europe; and 'Textura rotunda' – slightly condensed in southern Europe. Thus, the Italian and Spanish 'Textura rotunda' economizes in depth only, while the German and French 'Textura quadrata' economizes also in width. Both scripts have thick strokes; both as scripts, or as types cut in imitation of the scripts, are much larger in face than the corresponding sizes of Roman. Hence, on account of its 'Gothic' anceſtry, Fraktur shares in this advantage; hence, too, the firſt syſtematic application of the principle of economic rationalization is, owing to the faƐt that Jannon's experiment in 1621 was abortive, to be sought outside Roman.

It has been mentioned that the northern 'Textura' possesses a double economic advantage. So, too, does Fraktur. Neither Fuhrmann's Nuremberg undescribed new cutting (a large face 'Mittel') of 1616, nor Jannon's 'gros cicero' (so described) of 1621, is obviously less wide than the normal Romans – though, possibly, a tendency to condensation may be discerned in Fuhrmann's cutting 'Norimbergae fusa'. It is otherwise with 'Fraktur'. This, by its nature, is condensed; a point to which we shall return. Meanwhile, it muſt be recognized that, although the firſt literary mention of 'große' (signifying a larger than usual face on the body) occurs in Pater's *Dissertatio* of 1710, the process in 'Fraktur' of ſtill further shortening projeƐtors in order to save space in depth was at leaſt as old as 1678. A 'Große Mittel' was shown in the specimens of 'FraƐtur' (and Schwabacher without title) issued by Johann Erasmus Luther of Frankfurt. The same process adapted to Roman and Italic is to be seen in the 'Große Cicero Antiqua und Cursiv' exhibited in the specimen of J. P. Fievet, Frankfurt, 1682.

The earlieſt surviving specimen of Fraktur issued by the J. E. Luther (or any other Frankfurt) foundry is dated 1678. It exhibits fifteen Frakturs, of which the Mittel, Cicero, Garamond, and Petit sizes are all companioned by a 'Große' face, placed, very conveniently for comparison, in a parallel column. The sheet is evidence of a syſtematic attempt by Frankfurt to meet the demand created by Leipzig. There are signs, however, that Leipzig was intereſted, perhaps earlier than Frankfurt, in further exploiting the second economic advantage of Fraktur over Roman. It has been pointed out that Fraktur already saved space, as againſt Roman, in depth and width. At some time between 1616 and 1710, either at Frankfurt, Nuremberg, or Leipzig, there began the cutting of what the present-day trade would call an 'extra-condensed' Fraktur. Fuhrmann shows what he calls a 'Jungfrauschrift', which is extra-condensed. Pater's term for a similar effort is 'Neue längliche Leipziger Corpus' (i.e. the body size of the Fraktur).

THE DUTCH ROMANS

The trend to the use of the vernacular in books and especially in cheap books was joined by the invention, in Germany, of the weekly news-book. This was necessarily written in German and composed in Frak-tur, firſt in long lines. When, later, the *Avisos* and *Poſts* appeared in double-column, trade demand for extra-condensed type was in-evitable. More or less simultaneously, the increasing cult of the Bible and the multiplication of texts in double column ſtimulated the produ&ion of special Fraktur types in Germany and Roman types in Holland (and even in England) which were economic in two dimen-sions. Such Romans were much used in England, where similar condi-tions and demands arose during the Civil War. It cannot be said that these new, seventeenth-century Romans, economic in width as well as depth, were designed with much sense of ſtyle, or, even when cut by the moſt eſteemed engravers in Holland, display any great expertness.

The authentic Dutch national version of the Garamond Roman and Granjon Italic is handsomely exhibited in the *Proeven van Letteren, die gesneden ʒijn door Wylen Chriſtoffel van Dyck* (Sheet no. 12) issued in 1681 on the occasion of the sale by the widow of Daniel Elzevir of the founding material he had colle&ed (1629–80), not all of the punches of which were from the hand of Van Dyck. Moxon (and discerning critics since) regarded him as 'among lettering artiſts worthily accounted the beſt'. He also admired Van Dyck as a man and spent much time with him during his ſtay in Holland. 'The common consent of Book men as-sign the Garland to the Dutch letters as of late cut', wrote Moxon in 1683. The excellence of Van Dyck's engraving and the weight of Moxon's authority maintained the design in England, whose 'Book men' in the firſt half of the eighteenth century were equally ready to 'assign the Garland' to the same 'Dutch letters as of late cut'. On the

Continent at the end of the seventeenth century the Garamond design was already regarded as requiring revision. The Paris ſtyle which had dominated Europe for a century and a half was deemed out of date. The humaniſts of the reign of Francis I had been succeeded by the scientiſts under Louis XIV.

THE PARIS SCIENTIFIC TYPE, 1702

In 1692 Louis XIV authorized the creation of a new series of types for the exclusive use of the Imprimerie Royale. It is probable that security reasons contributed moſt powerfully to the decision; but, even so, the disciples of Descartes and Mersenne were pressing forward a pѕogramme to rationalize everything and, with the reſt, the forms that record and transmit thought. This involved a revolution in the types of the Royal Printing House. These included the Romans and Italics originated by Jannon at Sedan, and other older faces available to the general trade. The committee charged by the Académie des Sciences engaged in the conſtruɛtion of all the letters to be used in Richelieu's foundation upon a basis that might have aſtonished him. The patterns for the punch-cutter to follow were engraved on copper plates, each letter on a field divided into 2,304 squares.

The work was begun in 1692 and occupied years. The firſt specimen, in 16 point, was proofed in 1699 but the firſt book to be composed in the fount for which it was engraved did not appear until 1702. The 'Romain du Roi Louis XIV' was then publicly exhibited in a hiſtorical text. It was superbly composed, illuſtrated, printed and produced. The whole of the work on the *Médailles sur les principaux événements du règne de Louis le Grand* was superintended by the Académie des Inscriptions. The medals were from the hand of the greateſt of French portrait engravers, Gérard Edelinck (a Fleming from Antwerp), and the borders were by Jean Berain, 'dessinateur de la Chambre et du cabinet du Roi'. No book between the 'Gutenberg' Bible, the 1457 Psalter, and the Kelmscott Chaucer, is comparable with the *Médailles*. The objeɛtion that Aldus was not greatly interested in presswork is, unfortunately true. The *Polifilo* of 1499 is superb in illustration, but miserable in presswork, when compared, for example, with the best of Jenson.

Simultaneously with the *Médailles* there appeared the *Epreuve d'un nouveau caractère pour l'Imprimerie Royale. A Paris Gravé par Grandjean, graveur de l'Imprimerie Royale, Fevrier 1702*. Unfortunately the only evidence of the existence of this specimen is a type-facsimile executed (for what reason one cannot say) after 1750 or so. It is printed on wove paper, which was hardly possible in 1702.

THE NEW PARIS SERIF

The principal graphic novelty in the 'Romain du Roi' is the serif. Its horizontal and unbracketed structure symbolizes a complete break with the humanist calligraphic tradition. Also, the main strokes are thicker and the substrokes thinner than in the Aldine-Garamond-Granjon-Jannon design. While these two innovations are of great importance and vitally affected future typographical design, they are, by themselves, of no more than artistic significance. More important is the fact that in the 'Romain du Roi' some of the characters, when compared with the Aldine Romans, are slightly condensed; the projectors are proportionately reduced and, correspondingly, the height of a, c, e, and the rest of the normal lower case, is slightly increased. Briefly, therefore, the Paris type of 1699–1702 presents the first of a style that departed from the humanistic design that had dominated the Roman letter since 1495. It set a new style, that of a rationalist and economic design which went far to compromise the accepted theoretical basis of typography, which was that Roman lettering was a regularized, mechanized and disciplined aspect of calligraphy, in favour of the theory that printed lettering is so regularized, so mechanized and so disciplined as not rightly to be regarded as an aspect of calligraphy, but more truly as an aspect of epigraphy or chalcography. The presence in Paris of the greatest school of portrait engraving, and of the craftsmen who worked for the great writing-maſters, naturally assiſted this transition to the theory that a print of lettering should oſtensibly be an engraved and not a written form. This view of the artiſtic ſtatus of type was supported by the contemporary vogue for books of devotion printed from copper-plates finely engraved after models set by the beſt calligraphers of the day. It would occupy too much space here to discuss the influence of the engravers upon Italic and the approval given to the models of Alais by the Abbé Bignon.

Considered ſtyliſtically, the change from a calligraphic basis of lettering is of the utmoſt significance, since it led direƈtly to the ſtriking typographical effeƈts produced by Giambattiſta Bodoni. Although the relative economy in depth is slight, it exiſts; and while the degree of saving in width is even slighter it is again perceptible. There is also the slight increase in the height of the normal lower case to be considered. Finally, it should be remarked, the new horizontal serif entailed the raising of the capitals to the level of the horizontal serif of the ascenders, inſtead of, as in the Aldine Roman, to the lower level indicated by the dip of their diagonal serif. Thus, in the 'Romain du Roi' the capitals are taller than in all preceding Romans when used normally, though exceptions may be found in the sixteenth century. The theory underlying the conſtruƈtion of the 'Romain du Roi' is explained in the copious memorandum which Jaugeon prepared for the Académie des Sciences. He indulged himself so liberally that the text was considered too expensive to print, and has remained in manuscript to this day. This is regrettable.

Had Jaugeon's report been printed, with the magnificent geometrical diagrams engraved to accompany it, our terminology might have been rationalized and, for inſtance, our sixteenth-century terms 'Roman' and 'Italic' might have been superseded by the new terms 'Droit' and 'Penché'. The faƈt remains that the types created upon the rationaliſt theory of Louis XIV's scientific commission created the watershed whose exiſtence Fournier-le-Jeune, writing 1764–6, and soon to be mentioned, acknowledges in the diſtinƈtion he draws between 'ancien' and 'moderne'. As M. André Jammes shows in the course of his print [published 1962] of a series of documents on the origins of the Paris type, the measurement of the bodies and the establishment of their relations to each other was also part of that enterprise. In other words, the method of Louis XIV's reform of typography was more thoroughly scientific than was understood until the discoveries now reported. [See André Jammes, *La Réforme de la Typographie Royale sous Louis XIV – Le Grandjean*, Paris, 1962.]

The Commission thus opened the way for Fournier's point system promulgated as part of his conception of a 'nouvelle typographie' and necessitates a revision of his claims to have been the creator of the point system. It is true, however, that in 1737 Fournier published an elaboration of the system originated for the Imprimerie Royale as part of the monarch's plan to rationalize the *arts et métiers*. The first meeting of Louis XIV's commission was held in January 1693 at the residence, and under the presidency, of the Abbé Bignon. The Table of the 'Proportions des Caractères de l'Imprimerie Royalle' was drawn up by the Père Truchet *c.* 1693.

THE 'MODERN' FACE

The German approximation toward what Pater calls the 'neue Schnitt' and Fournier the 'moderne' may, or may not, be independent of the 'Romain du Roi'. In the present state of knowledge there is reason to think that the German rationalist approach to Roman is a response less to the Roman example of Paris than to the Fraktur example of Leipzig. What is certain is that the task of assimilating Roman to Fraktur in terms of the relation of thick and thin strokes, of the new proportioning of the projectors to the normal lower case, was committed to the punch-cutters of Leipzig and Frankfurt during the first quarter of the eighteenth century.

The process is to be seen in the sheet honorifically entitled *Verzeichniss derer Holländischen Schrifften* collected by Wolfgang Dietrich Ehrhardt of Leipzig, whose successors published the specimen about 1720 (as Mori judges). Here is what the trade would now describe as a 'series' of related sizes of condensed, large face Romans and Italics, the whole harmoniously designed in accordance with rationaliſt, economic principles. The design is also notable for the extra emphasis of the thick ſtrokes, an additional approximation to the superior ſtrength of Fraktur. In other respeċts, Ehrhardt's faces show no innovation; their ſtyle is uniformly conservative.

The firſt to impose conscious ſtyle upon the Ehrhardt proportions was the Nuremberg punch-cutter, Johann Michael Fleischman. Having served his apprenticeship to Hartwig, the leading typefounder of his native city, Fleischman migrated to Frankfurt, spent a year in the Luther foundry, and thence went to Holland, where Uytwerf employed him in 1732 and Enschedé from 1734. It is only necessary here to perceive that their designs are all condensed founts and that, in comparison with all its predecessors, the Fleischman design has one marked charaċteriſtic. The 'Romain du Roi' is geometrical throughout. There is nothing personal about it. Designed to accord with the findings of a scientific commission, the face fully preserves the virtues of logic and consiſtency. Fleischman's design, while following the general scale of the Paris founts, is more condensed and increases the contraſts between the thicks and thins. The serifs to the lower case are of the diagonal and not of the horizontal type, but the capitals correspond to the Paris formula. In design the serifs to the capitals are of novel weight and design. As a whole, Fleischman's founts represent the firſt personal, individualiſt interpretation of Roman and Italic. Fraktur had long been patient of personal interpretation. On the other hand, whereas Fraktur, in the hands of the Leipzig engravers, not only preserved but even exaggerated its calligraphic basis, the Roman in the hands of Fleischman is essentially an engraved letter. His Fraktur, or Duits, is also an engraved letter, owing little or nothing to calligraphy. Between 1732, when Fleischman began cutting for Herman Uytwerf (who, apparently, deserves the credit for encouraging Fleischman in his modernism), and 1743, when his material descended to Isaac and Johannes Enschedé, the design won recognition as the moſt advanced Roman and Italic in commerce. The 'Romain du Roi' was ſtriċtly re-

served to the Imprimerie Royale; Fleischman's Romans and Italics had
Europe before them. The Paris trade, therefore, was bound to take notice of the 'Goût Hollandais'.

THE RISE OF ENGLISH TYPEFOUNDING

Contemporary with this work on the Continent, from the beginning
almoſt the sole source of supply for the English trade, was the rise of
the moſt capable engraver London had known for a century and a half:
William Caslon I (1692–1766). He was encouraged, some time before
1722, by William Bowyer to set up as a trade-typefounder. He produced, in 1734, 'A specimen by W. Caslon, Letter-Founder, in Iron-
monger Row, Old-Street, London' exhibiting a fine series of titlings,
upper and lower case founts from canon to nonpareil; Black-Letters,
exotics and flowers.

The encouragement given to Caslon by Bowyer was the English
equivalent of the encouragement given to Fleischman by Uytwerf in
Holland. The results were wholly different. By 1744, when Enschedé
published the firſt full specimen of Fleischman's founts, they had superseded the old faces, including not only the Garamonds and Granjons,
but the Van Dycks which had been the model for Moxon and Caslon.

Consequently, the provision in England of a full series of what soon
became an English national version of what Moxon called 'the late
Dutch cutting', had the effeſt of saddling the country with a ſtyle that
was out of date before it was completed. The massive contribution of
Caslon forced British book produſtion into a conservative 'old face'
preference that was maintained for two generations; was deſtined to be
revived in the nineteenth century; and ſtill receives the 'common consent of Book men'. Contemporary English colleſtors continue to 'as-
sign the Garland' to the 'old face' types. The elaboration of a modern
theory of letter design applicable to contemporary typography found
no place in the English publishing trade of the mid-eighteenth century.

There were not wanting amateurs of early typography. After Maittaire, Joseph Ames is the moſt prominent name in English bibliogra-

phy. His *Typographical Antiquities* (London, 1749), as its sub-title claims, brought together a 'Historical Account of Printing in England: with some Memoirs of our Antient Printers, and a Register of the Books printed by them, from 1471 to 1600'. It was a highly influential book, and more explicit on the typographical side than was then to be expected from a widely cultivated bookman or professional librarian. Ames was, in fact, a professional tradesman and collector. He had continental literature upon which to draw. At this time, several French historical works were read in England: Jean de La Caille, *Histoire de l'imprimerie et de la librairie* (Paris, 1689), which is still of value to historians, and André Chevillier's *L'origine de l'Imprimerie de Paris* (Paris, 1694). These, however, though important for annalistic and literary purposes, throw no light on typographical variations.

FOURNIER-LE-JEUNE'S 'MANUEL', PARIS, 1764–6

It is otherwise with the work of a notable French author who illuminated the trade in the eighteenth century, and reformed Parisian typefounding. The *Manuel Typographique* of Fournier-le-Jeune (2 vols., Paris, 1764, 1766) is informed with knowledge that could only have been gained in practical work. Fournier had already produced a magnificent oblong folio *Modèles des Caractères de l'Imprimerie* in 1742. The invention and craftsmanship of this album, whose format surpassed that pioneered by Ernesti, are alike superb. The mass of specimens, roman as well as exotic, in the *Manuel* and the accompanying historical text documenting the sixteenth and seventeenth centuries is of unique value to historians of typographical style. The collection of data, notwithstanding that it would be a gross exaggeration to describe it as rich, had never before been accumulated. Many of the Garamond and Granjon originals were provided by Fournier's elder brother who never himself issued a specimen of his uniquely rich foundry, which was originated by Guillaume le Bé I. The specimens are the more valuable since they provide alphabets. If the *Manuel* had, in some respects, been anticipated by Ernesti, yet Fournier's appendix II to the volume II is new. The text, unique in value, sketches the hiſtory of the principal foundries in Europe and ranks as a pioneer work on typefounding; though it is juſt to remember that Moxon anticipated Fournier in his description of the manual operations of founding, caſting, etc. Fournier provides two paragraphs on the British foundries, which, as he truly says, were few, but the confused liſt he provides shows he was misinformed about Oxford.

More important and reliable are Fournier's references to Dutch foundries. He succeeds in being polite about Fleischman, and describes him as a very skilful letter-cutter. He notes that the Enschedés, having bought the Wetſtein foundry, benefited from the labours and talent of the above-mentioned Fleischman, whose services they had attraƈted. This is all that Fournier finds room for in his *Manuel* (II, see appendix II). But, as Mr Harry Carter has pointed out, he entertained, even as late as 1756, positive objeƈtions to the application of economic princi-ples to letter-design, which art should, he evidently thought, be left to men of taſte. 'The descendants of the Elzevirs are more shopkeepers than artiſts. They judge books by the profits they make. Not content with the superb rounded types which showed the good taſte of their forbears, they have procured a new variety more pleasing to the com-mercial mentality. The desire to economize upon the space which a well-made letter has a right to occupy has led them deliberately to ac-quire types of a cramped, ſtarved look, so that they may get more and more lines to the page.' Thus writes Fournier-le-Jeune in his 'Lettre sur l'Imprimerie' in the *Journal des Sçavans* of 1756.

FOURNIER'S SCIENTIFIC POINT SYSTEM

As will be proved by the examples which the Corpus will place before the reader, Fournier, who had begun as early as 1742 to assimilate the lessons to be drawn from the 'Romain du Roi', had cut a number of types on its proportions. His *Manuel* of 1764–6 shows a number of con-densed and extra-condensed Romans and Italics, cut by his own hand, with the intention of satisfying those who wished to 'get more and more lines to the page'. In other words, Fournier found irresiŝtible the scientific, economic tendency initiated in Paris by the Imprimerie Royale in 1702, independently initiated at Leipzig by Ehrhardt before 1720, and given an individuality at Amŝterdam and Haarlem by Fleischman after 1727; the ŝtyle known in Paris as the 'Goût Hollandais'.

Although he respeĉted under pressure the proportions of the 'Romain du Roi' he was no believer in the application of mathematical method to the design of the letter. On the other hand, Fournier was a profound believer in the application of scientific methods to the measurements of the body upon which his type faces were caŝt. Whereas he rejeĉted Jaugeon's idea of designing a face on the basis of a field divided into 2,304 squares, Fournier with no less regard for geometry applied his scientific mind not to the mathematics of the face but to the scale of the bodies. He arranged his bodies in a division of 144ths, or points, so that the smalleŝt would be 5 and the largeŝt would be 96 points. In other words he rationalized a situation which, he said, amounted to chaos. No one body was related to another. His remedy was 'l'invention des Points typographiques. Ce n'eŝt autre chose que la division des corps de Caraĉtères par degrés égaux et determinés, que j'appelle Points. Par ce moyens on connoîtra au juŝte les degrés de diŝtance et les rapports des corps.'

This ŝtandardizing of the relation of one body to another was Fournier's greateŝt invention; for, although regulations for the bookselling and printing trade made in 1723 successfully dealt with some of the anomalies in the trade (as, for example, differing heights-to-paper), the *Conseil* did not succeed in its effort to ŝtandardize type bodies, and it remained for Fournier, in 1737, to devise an efficient syŝtem. It prepared the way for the exiŝting Didot and American point syŝtems. The Fournier syŝtem continues in use in certain offices in Belgium.

It is to be admitted that the examples in the Corpus will hardly allow the inveŝtigator to make close mathematical measurements of the bodies of any of the small sizes of the types shown. As Fournier was well aware, the damped paper on which the proofs or prints were made shrinks in drying. Also, in reproduction by collotype, the process used to reproduce the specimens in this Corpus, there is a risk of shrinking. Hence, it is to be understood that the utility of the specimens in the Corpus stops short at absolute scientific reproduction of the original size of the print, even if the original itself should present an exact print of the type.

The process of rationalization in France may be followed in the later specimens of the Imprimerie Royale (and its successor the Imprimerie Imperiale) and of several members of the great dynasty of Didot, the Lorraine family which became interested in bookselling at the end of the seventeenth century. François Ambroise Didot (1730–1804) was mainly responsible for superseding Fournier's point-system by his calculations. As the Didot family pressed forward the supply of condensed faces for France, the same process is to be seen in Germany and elsewhere on the Continent. The old Aldine pattern was completely discarded by the third quarter of the eighteenth century.

THE TYPES OF BASKERVILLE, 1754

In England the continuing vogue of Caslon's types maintained the traditional proportions, and the Great Primer and Pica Roman and Italic shown on the *Specimen by John Baskerville of Birmingham, in the County of Warwick, Letter-Founder and Printer, MDCCLIV*, are hardly more than tentative departures from the traditional relations of depth and width. It is an important fact, however, that his descenders (g, p, q, etc.) are shorter than Caslon's. Baskerville's most obvious innovations are of artistic importance, as might be expected in a type cut by a practising writing-master. The origins of his style, which is individual in type, are to be found in the earlier copy-books of George Shelley and John Clark (1708). These prove Baskerville's style to be less than individual in script, and rather derivative; for which, of course, his letters are none the worse. The rationalization of the stress of the circular sorts, which began in England with the writing-masters, is a significant innovation in the development of Baskerville's typographical lettering. He did not follow it up with an economic rationalization of the width of the letters. It is curious that, although condensed lettering is to be found in the copper-engraved writing books of the period 1690–1710, their example had no effect on the punch-cutters. The copper engravers' condensed letters achieved a brilliant presence on the page of the *Horace* which John Pine completed within the years 1733 and 1737. The lettering of this work is a remarkably fine specimen of condensed designing and an absolute masterpiece of consistent engraving. It makes an important artistic contribution but, while manifesting a proper discontent with the face that continued to retain the 'Garland' of the booksellers, Pine's condensed lettering was bound to fail. It is simply not good enough as a design.

Baskerville, so far from encouraging condensation, slightly extended his characters. For him type was type, and he was too impressed with the example of 'Mr Caslon' who was 'an Artist, to whom the Republic of Learning has great obligations; his ingenuity has left a fairer copy for my emulation, than any other master'. In Britain in the third quarter of the eighteenth century (not merely in London), it is obvious that the trade of supplying type to printers was increasing with the expansion of newspaper publishing since the first London daily newspaper, the *Daily Courant* of 1702, opened up an entirely new category of typographical production.

TENTATIVE ECONOMIC DESIGN OF THE FIRST LONDON NEWSPAPER TYPES FROM 1665

That is to say, the first daily newspaper created a use for type not hitherto available to the cutters of punches and casters of type. The paper was set in double column like the *Oxford Gazette* founded in 1665. Passing mention of the *Gazette* was made above. It is now desirable to point out that this cavalier, twice-weekly sheet was the first of all English newspapers, as distinct from newsbooks, and that it was 'Published by Authority'. It was a half-sheet in folio, set in double column and the firſt regular publication of the kind to be so set. The type area is 5½ in. × 9½ in. and the size of letter is bourgeois with unnecessarily long de-scenders, while condensed for the purpose to an admirable degree; in faᶜt, the face is extra-condensed. Its hiſtory would be worth knowing. The type area of the *Daily Courant* is 6 ⁵⁄₁₆ in. × 12 in. and the type is a long primer, full on the body but not otherwise diſtinᶜtive. Like the type of the *Oxford*, later *London Gaʒette*, the cutting is rough. This is not important. The queſtion to ask is why should the *Gaʒette* type of 1665 be extra-condensed and the *Courant* type of 1702 be normal?

It paid Bible publishers in Holland to use narrow-bodied types and so save space, but it does not necessarily pay a newspaper to employ a condensed type for its text, and in any case unless forced by competi-tion it will usually choose a round type for its advertisements. George Larkin's thrice weekly *Poſt Boy* (1695) and Richard Baldwin's *Poſt Man* (1723) are found using condensed type, probably from the same source as that of the *London Gaʒette*. The praᶜtice did not laſt.

It is not to be overlooked that when Joseph Fry of Briſtol eſtablished his foundry in 1764, his partner was William Pine who was the pub-lisher of a newspaper: the Briſtol *Gaʒette*. Isaac Moore was the manager of the foundry, conduᶜtor of the business, and its designer. A *Specimen by Isaac Moore & Co. Letter-Founders, in Briſtol, 1766* provides types that show the inspiration of Baskerville and preserve his round proportions. And this remained the rule for books and newspaper composition until after the end of the eighteenth century. The economic faᶜtor is not re-sponsible for condensing the width. This requires recutting the punches of all charaᶜters. As the German founders had discovered much earlier, it was far easier to reduce the length of the projeᶜtors.

SYSTEMATIC ECONOMIC DESIGN IN LONDON, 1742

The firſt syſtematic economy in depth observable in England is to be seen in *A Specimen by W. Caslon, Letter-Founder, in Chiswel-ſtreet, Lon-don, 1742*, which exhibits alternate Pica, Small Pica, Long Primer, Brevier and Nonpareil bodies. In other words, the syſtem was adapted to all sizes below English. By 1785 the only exception was Pearl, which, as the laſt cut, was arranged to fill the body.

The adoption by the Caslon firm of the principle of cutting a 'Grobe' or 'Gros Œil' face as an alternative to the normal face with normal projeƈtors on a normal body, is of considerable economic significance, but it does not appear to have caused any discussion, comment, or even mention. But this is because the literature on printing in English since Moxon was purely antiquarian. Praƈtical literature had not flourished. England lacked a Fournier-le-Jeune.

In 1729 there was announced, as to appear in parts, *The General Hiſtory of Printing by S. Palmer, Printer.* The work was to be 'Printed for the Author, and sold at his Printing-House in Bartholomew-close', etc. It was an unfortunate enterprise. Firſt, the author died and the book began being 'Printed for the Author, and sold by his Widow at his late Printing-House in Bartholomew-close', etc. The scale of the book was reduced, much matter was dropped and the display of founts of moſt languages, promised by Palmer, was omitted. The text was compiled from Mallinkrodt, Chevillier, De la Caille and Watson. The common ſtate of typographical criticism is exemplified in the seƈtion on Wynkyn de Worde in which Palmer follows Bagford. He provides as specimens the Roman types which Caslon used; a Double Pica and a Great Primer of the Oxford series – which Mr Harry Carter rightly thinks were cut by Peter Walpergen. As to De Worde's black-letter, Palmer (or, rather, George Psalmanazar, on the basis of Palmer's notes) shows a two-line Great Primer and a Great Primer which he could easily do, since 'the very letter he [de Worde] made use of, is the same us'd by all the Printers in London to this day; and I believe were ſtruck from his puncheons'. There is not much more to say about the book, for the widow confided the editorship to the eager and careless hands of George Psalmanazar, the notorious French adventurer and literary impoſtor. The work, when completed in 1733, was full of errors.

England was far from superseding Moxon; ſtill farther from prepar-

ing to produce the equivalent of a *Manuel Typographique*, or to appreciate the importance, as Fournier was conſtrained to do, of the economic
faƈtor in type-design. The taſte for fine printing that Baskerville had
ſtimulated remained conservative. Novelty did not enter into the ſtyle
that was ensured by the brothers Andrew and Robert Foulis, who had
been printers to the University of Glasgow since 1743. They used the
types of Alexander Wilson, founder in the same city, who retained the
Baskerville proportions. In 1785 the Foulis brothers produced a folio
edition in three volumes of Pope, with the Glasgow types. Wilson sent
out his firſt specimen in 1772, long after he had cut a Greek for the
Homer that Foulis published in 1756. The Wilson types, Roman and
other, were all of the Baskerville proportions, and thus were equally
ruled by 'Taſte'. This was ariſtocratic in the caſt of Baskerville, and the
academicism of the Foulis made no change. Moreover, the pedigree of
the types of both Baskerville and Foulis was insular, though Baskerville
could go to Paris engravers for his illuſtrations.

INFLUENCE OF THE DIDOTS ABROAD

There was ſtill not available in England a *Manuel* such as Fournier's that
would digeſt, for the benefit of the eighteenth-century colleƈtor, bookseller or printer, the information that French connoisseurs had long possessed. Giambattiſta Bodoni (1740–1813) had learned much from
Fournier before he ventured upon his luxurious *Manuale Tipografico* of
1788. It muſt be admitted, however, that Fournier's *Manuel* was not, as a
piece of composition, an impressive piece, or intended as such. His specimen of 1742 is speƈtacular. But Bodoni learned everything from the
Manuel and surpassed it in size, magnificence and even luxury. The Romans and other types here displayed were conceived for the composition
of *éditions de luxe*. The designs were new; but even Bodoni, as a court
printer, was slow to adopt the principle of condensation. However,
Fournier and the several members of the Didot family, whose colleƈtive
output of punches was prodigious, exerted a determining influence.

Although the Didots alternatively thinned and thickened the mainstroke, they consistently narrowed the average width of the characters. In other words, they made condensation of the alphabet a principle of design. It is to this family that we owe the canonization of the condensed letter, and the editions and types of its various members, notably François-Ambroise (1730–1804), Pierre François (1732–95), Pierre (1760–1853), Firmin (1764–1836) to whom Bodoni, in his later career, after 1790, was indebted.

THE VOGUE OF BODONI

That Bodoni was employed by the London booksellers to print editions of Walpole, Gray and Thomson was significant. While he was still under the influence of the *Manuel Typographique*, and, ten years after the death of its author, there appeared in London the first special history of the houses that had supplied the type for the English trade, the *Dissertation upon English Typographical Founders and Foundries* of the Rev. Edward Rowe Mores. It is a pity that he never read the history of the French founders and foundries that Fournier provided. Mores, as an opinionated and insular egoist, limited himself to matters in which he was personally interested, and of which he had personal knowledge. He was a true English antiquary, and his book is of fundamental importance to the details of the transfer of punches and matrices. Yet it has no palaeographical significance. Neither Ames, Herbert nor Mores observed distinctions between founts, however considerably they might vary in the trained eyes of a Fournier. It was he who, by the distinction of terms 'ancienne' and 'moderne' in respect of Roman and Italic, pointed the way towards a typographical nomenclature which, in fact, the trade followed in France. The necessity for such a distinction had not yet been seen in England. Nor, despite Mores, was there any wide interest in type. It is curious that the inclusion of the specimen of William Caslon in Ephraim Chambers's *Cyclopedia* (3rd edition 1740) did not then advance typographical discrimination.

Although Herbert's expansion (1785–90) of Ames advanced the understanding and appreciation of books in the bibliophilic sense, he did not describe the types used in English printing, otherwise than to say that they were either black-letter, roman or italic. The librarians of the time did not essay to give the inquisitive reader a clear idea of the origin and appearance of the type he had before him. Nor, indeed, are librarians quick to do so today. The attempt to be precise in the description of type awaited the emergence of a modern bibliographer.

The situation in Ames's time, both in England and on the Continent, was that, notwithstanding the books of Ernesti, who was a printer-typefounder, and Fournier-le-Jeune who was a founder, librarians and scholars had not learned the art of examining types closely. In effect, the methods of classification invented by Mabillon and elaborated by Toustain, Tassin and others for the study of manuscripts, had passed unnoticed by those occupied with the study of printed books. The nearest approach in typography to the terms used in palaeography was made by Fournier-le-Jeune. Generally, therefore, while the science of palaeography, as we understand it, existed, the counterpart in bibliography did not.

TYPOGRAPHICAL INNOVATIONS
OF JOHN BELL, LONDON, 1788

It has been seen that William Caslon I and his successors from 1734, John Baskerville from 1757, Cottrell in 1760, Moore in 1766, Wilson in 1772, departed far from the proportions established by Aldus from 1495 and adopted by Garamond in 1545. In 1787 John Bell, a London publisher, inspired by the example of the Imprimerie Royale, François-Ambroise Didot, and of other printing houses in Paris, began a type-foundry where he procured the cutting of a fount of the Continental proportions, that is, of large face on the body and condensed in width; thus making a dual economy of space. The serifs are of the Aldine pattern and in the other respects the face looks conservative. Bell's face, engraved by Richard Auſtin, ranks as the firſt of the 'modern' faces to be cut in England. *A Specimen of the firſt Set of types completed under his* [*Bell's*] *Directions* is dated May 1788; the sole example of which is with the Anisson collection in the Bibliothèque Nationale. The specimen exhibits the design in two sizes, English and Paragon. The present text is composed in Bell's English. One of the novelties in the fount is the set of 'modern' or 'ranging' numerals. No doubt other specimens were circulated in Paris by Bell. It would be too much, however, to say that they occasioned any particular intereſt in that city.

It was a year later, however, that the firſt liſt of typefounders' 'specimens' was compiled. In that year Auguſtin Martin Lottin published his *Catalogue Chronologique des Libraires et des Libraires-Imprimeurs de Paris*. It includes a 'Notice chronologique des Libraires, Imprimeurs et Artiſtes qui se sont occupés de la Gravure et de la Fonte des Caractères Typographiques'. This is the initial ſtep in the bibliography of the ſtudy of the alphabetical design that ultimately appears on the printed pages from the sixteenth century. Lottin was a bookseller in 1746 at the age of 20, and became Imprimeur du duc de Berry in 1760, to the Ville de Paris in 1768 and even to Louis XVI in 1775. The *Modèle des Caractères de l'Imprimerie de Lottin,* which is mentioned by Lepreux as having been printed in 1761, is, apparently, loſt. In 1781 another edition was published. So much for the firſt attempt to enumerate typefounders' 'specimens'. Lottin's 'Notice', however, is essentially a contribution to the hiſtory of the founders, and only accidentally of use to the hiſtory of the type-designs they cut, caſt and sold.

FIRST BIBLIOPHILIC
ENQUIRIES INTO EARLY TYPOGRAPHY

The inveſtigation of printing types, as such, quite properly began with the ſtudy of the books printed in the fifteenth century. As noted above, public attention was not drawn to typography as such until 1640 when certain German cities celebrated the second centenary of the invention. In France Richelieu founded the Imprimerie Royale in Paris, which exerted a powerful influence upon ſtyle. It did not create in France any immediate intereſt in the close ſtudy of the work of the early printers and the types they used.

Technical and literary intereſt in early printing followed from this German cuſtom of celebrating the anniversary of the invention of printing with movable type. The cuſtom was invented to celebrate the second centenary of the art itself, which was taken to have been invented in 1440. Bernard von Mallinkrodt's *De ortu ac progressu artis typographicae Dissertatio Hiſtorica* (Cologne, 1640) is the firſt attempt to eſtablish the priority of the invention for Germany. He colleĉts information about early printers and has much to say of Plantin and his *Biblia Regia*. But Mallinkrodt, as the dean of the Cathedral Chapter of Münſter in Weſtphalia, does not forget to chronicle the Complutensian Polyglot and to praise its initiator, Ximenez, and its printer, Brocar. Mallinkrodt's *Dissertatio* is the firſt attempt to provide a hiſtory of the art of printing, and some of the operations it involves. He was no engineer like Moxon, and hardly mentions the mechanics. As to type, he knows of the varieties and appreciates the '[litteras] Italicas quas vocant' (p. 105).

Further literary notice of early printed books came two or three years later with Johann Saubert's *Hiſtoria bibliothecae Norimbergensis. . .accessit appendix De Inventore Typographiae, itemque Catalogus librorum proximis ab inventione annis usque ad A.C. 1500 editorum*. This little book (2½ in. × 4½ in.) liſts titles of the fifteenth century, beginning in 1466, to be found in the City library which was founded in 1530. Saubert's appendix is the firſt attempt to compile a liſt of the works of the early printers. It appeared at Nuremberg in 1643. The author was a paſtor at St Sebald's church, where 250 years later he was to find a worthy successor in Georg Wolfgang Panzer, to be mentioned in due time.

Ten years later the immensely erudite and energetic Jesuit, Philippe Labbé (1607–67), compiled his *Nova Bibliotheca manuscriptorum librorum* (Paris, 1653). Among other ſtudies Labbé pursued Byzantine hi&ory, Greek and Latin philology, and was continually searching for 'sources'. The use of the words 'typographiae incunabula' to describe books printed in the childhood of the art occurs in Mallinkrodt's *De ortu ac progressu artis typographicae* in his chapter 'Diversae opiniones de Inventione Typographiae, deque illis indicium' (p. 5), but the word 'incunabula' was slow to enter the language of bibliography. Labbé's *Nova Bibliotheca* contains, at appendix 9, a li& of fir& printed editions in the Royal Library at Paris 'quae ante centum et quinquaginta annos, in ipsis paene typographiae incunabulis, prodierunt'. This is the term adopted by the next generation of bibliographers and appears in the title of the fir& separate publication on the subje&: Cornelius à Beughem, *Incunabula typographiae sive catalogus librorum scriptorum que proximis ab inventione*...(Am&elodami, 1688). This little book (of the popular Elzevir format) is an inventory of incunabula arranged under authors. Beughem's preliminary essay praises Labbé.

In England in 1717 the lives of the E&iennes and others were narrated in the *Hi&oria typographorum aliquot Parisiensium vitas et libros comple&ens* by Michael Maittaire (1668–1747), of a Huguenot refugee family domiciled in London. The volume, *Typis Guglielmi Bowyer*, is handsomely produced in an unidentified Roman, probably of Dutch origin. Maittaire's much more significant work was the &udy of typography, *Annales typographici*, which, by li&ing incunabula according to place, chronicles the development and dispersion of the art from its origins to 1664. The work began publishing in Holland 1719, and was completed in 1741 and was the basis for much later work.

A significant advance in the cataloguing of incunabula was made by the learned French friar, François Xavier Laire (1738–1801), whose superiors, perhaps unfortunately, prevailed upon Pius VI to dispense him from accepting an appointment to the Vatican Library. Laire went in&ead to serve in the library of the Cardinal (he was excommunicated and expelled from the College in 1791) Loménie de Brienne, for the sake of the great colle&ion of books his position had enabled him to amass by the suppression of so many convents.

Laire was eminently fitted to catalogue the incunabula. He had proved his quality with the publication of *Specimen hiſtoricum typographiae Romanae XV saeculi* (Romae, 1778) in which, for the firſt time, the types used by the early Roman printers are noted. Two of them are illuſtrated by a copper-plate facsimile, the firſt of which is the type that Sweynheym and Pannartz engraved for the Laĉtantius of 1465. Of this Laire shows a few lines. It is rather a caricature than a facsimile of the original. But Laire's method was correĉt. It was the skill that was inadequate. The craftsmanship of the engravers of Rome was evidently, at this time, not of the superior quality available in Paris to Mabillon in 1681; and the plate remains ſtriking teſtimony that all scientific criticism of typographical variations awaited the invention of the photographic camera. The palaeographers were also handicapped, but to a lesser degree, since so many of the originals upon which they worked are written in script two or three times the size of the letters used in printed books. It is important to observe that, had Laire possessed the facilities available to later generations, his essay on early Roman typography would have been a considerable landmark in the scientific ſtudy of the art.

The revival of English intereſt in her Saxon paſt, so well described in David Douglas's *English Scholars* (London, 1939, and often reprinted), created principally by George Hickes and Humphrey Wanley inspired, together with the example of Mabillon, a new intereſt in charters and manuscripts and the hands in which they were written.

Thomas Aſtle (1735–1803), a disciple of Hickes, brought out his *Origin and Progress of Writing* (London) in 1784. He is entitled to respeĉt as the virtual founder of the serious ſtudy of Latin palaeography in England. The second edition of Aſtle (London, 1806) is ſtill of use, since the many illuſtrations are accurately engraved. Anglo-Saxon and Celtic ſtudies were favoured by John Obadiah Weſtwood (1805–93). Private means enabled him to follow antiquarian hobbies. He excelled firſt in drawing, minutely, inseĉts; secondly, illuminations in manuscripts. His *Palaeographia Sacra Piĉtoria* (London, 1843) shows him to be chiefly interested in ornamental script and book illustration, and illumination.

EARLY SCIENTIFIC STUDY
OF EARLY TYPOGRAPHY OR INCUNABULA

The first application of scientific method to the study of early typography was made in Germany ten years after Laire's monograph was published in Rome. In 1789 the librarian of the Benedictine Abbey of SS. Ulrich and Afra at Augsburg, Dom Placidus Braun (1756–1829), completed the two volumes of his catalogue of the Abbey's printed books and listed the manuscripts in six volumes between 1791 and 1796. The printed books, which concern us, occupy two volumes of his *Notitia historico-litteraria de libris ab artis typographicae inventione usque ad annum 1479–1500 impressis*. The volumes are well arranged and set up by the printer Veith in Augsburg. Braun was a disciple of 'lumen ordinis nostri splendidissimum magnus Mabillonius' as the author describes him in the dedication to the Abbot of SS. Ulrich and Afra. On the title page to volume I Braun adds 'Accedunt VIII Tabulae Aereae sexaginta primorum typographorum alphabeta continentes'. These plates, placed at the end of the volume (volume II has three tabulae), display the types of Mentelin, Eggestein, Bämler and other German printers, etc.; also Ulrich Han of Rome and W. da Spira of Venice. Of these plates Braun was properly proud. He knew he was to some extent an innovator in bibliographical method. In order to aid better understanding of the subject, above all to allow comparison, he had caused to be engraved sixty alphabets (there were sixteen in volume II) 'tam maiora quam minora' [in upper and lowercase], a me delineata incidi curavi (devera characterum notitione erudirent)' that others beside himself might have the benefit of a true idea of the types.

The plates are elegantly engraved after excellent tracings which provide an authentic reproduction of the originals. It is important to note, and Braun deserves all credit for it, that the specimens are in alphabetical form, for example, the capitals and lowercase; three of Mentelin's types generously if not completely set out, that is, with ligatures, accented and other 'special' sorts. The drudgery of labour in accomplishing a work of this order, even with the aid of photographs, will be appreciated only by those who have attempted anything of the kind. It is not surprising that the method was not followed by other bibliographers until Blades grappled with the problem raised by the analysis of Caxton's types. He had photography and lithography at his command. Braun, it muſt be allowed, had made full use of the calligraphic resources of the Abbey of SS. Ulrich and Afra, and was thus enabled to surpass the *Specimen* of Laire, whose intereſt shifted from Rome to Venice.

Laire's *Serie delle ediʒione aldine* (Pisa, 1790) is the firſt attempt at a bibliography of Aldus. His more bulky work is the *Index librorum ab inventa typographia ad annum* 1500; *chronologice dispositus* (Sens, 1791) a bibliographical ſtatement of the contents of de Brienne's library. The *Index* was turned, by accident, into a sale catalogue and rushed out with a multitude of errors by the printer, Tarbé. However, in numerous inſtances Laire notices the length of columns (number of lines), pages, signatures and other physical features of the incunabula. He ranks as the firſt bibliographer to appreciate typography as an art as well as a technique. Laire, however, only diſtinguishes two groups of type, Gothic and Roman. His *Index* remains the catalogue of a specific colleſtion.

A general ſtudy of the incunabula was simultaneously undertaken by the Lutheran Paſtor, Georg Wolfgang Panzer (1729–1805). He produced the firſt volume of his *Annales Typographici* at Nuremberg in 1793. While a narrator like Maittaire, Panzer's *Annales* were more than a chronicle of the art, and a gazetteer of its expansion. Panzer, like Laire, perceived the importance of the letter-forms. He identified unsigned books by grouping them according to the individual typedesign in which they were composed, and next compared them with the signed books. This enabled him to credit unsigned books to the Strassburg presses of Mentelin, Eggeſtein, Husner and Flach.

Panzer completed the eleventh and laſt volume of his *Annales* in 1803, his final volumes having extended his reach from 1501 to 1536. His moſt significant contribution, in point of method, lies in his pressing forward the pioneer application, slight as it was, by Laire of comparative typography to the whole incunable period. The syſtem seems elementary to present-day typographers, as Mabillon's would have done to the generation of palaeographers that followed him; but it was too new in Panzer's time in respe჆t of printed books for him to find an audience that appreciated it. No further application of the comparative method to typography appears to have been made until half a century after Panzer; which is not surprising in view of the ſtate of Europe in general, and Germany in particular, from 1802. The Napoleonic age was not propitious for hiſtorical ſtudies.

ENGLISH BIBLIOPHILY AFTER JOHN BELL

It has been seen that in England Baskerville's new types and sumptuous publications had led Bell and others to emulate his example. The creation and eſtablishment of a taſte in England for artiſtry in book-produ჆tion spanned the period of Baskerville's quarto *Milton* of 1758 and Bell's o჆tavo *Shakespeare* of 1795. The moſt ambitious of these proje჆ts was the *Shakespeare* which began publishing in 1790 by Boydell and Nicol, and printing by William Bulmer, and took twenty years to complete. The punches for the types used for composition at the Shakespeare Press were cut by William Martin. He was carefully inſtru჆ted to respe჆t the beſt models; and the moſt admired of that day were those of Baskerville and Bodoni. The result is a new Roman on continental lines, condensed like Bell's, but having the heavier mainſtrokes that Bodoni had introduced. Martin had learnt his art in Baskerville's employment and the ſtyle, as diſtin჆t from the proportions of the Shakespeare fount, remain English. This is especially true of the italic. For a work so sumptuous as the *Shakespeare*, any attention to economy was unnecessary. On the other hand, a new Roman cut in London at the end of the eighteenth century was required to be 'fashionable' and at this time such a type avoided being round like Baskerville's, but was condensed like Bodoni's and had his stronger contrasts.

The trend of 'taste' (for such it was) at the end of the eighteenth century inspired the abandonment for fine book-work of the kind of type with which England had been familiar in its literature from Shakespeare to Pope and which the next century was correctly to describe as 'old face'.

ENGLISH SCIENTIFIC BIBLIOGRAPHY,

ADAM CLARKE, 1817–26

In London the first decade of the nineteenth century was distinguished, in the bibliographical sense, by the works of the Rev. Dr Adam Clarke (1762?–1832). An ardent Methodist, and three times president of the Conference, Clarke was the author of a host of theological books, pamphlets and sermons. His *magnum opus* was the *Commentary on the Holy Scriptures* (8 vols., 1817–26). In 1802–4 appeared the six volumes (in 12mo) of his *Bibliographical Dictionary* and in 1806 the two volumes, in similar format, of his *Bibliographical Miscellany*. These works form a history of printing, including an alphabetical list of the towns into which printing was introduced and the dates of such introduction; also a list of the authors who had written on the subject and a catalogue of the first editions of works desirable in a library, for example, the Bible, the Liturgy, general literature. Much valuable information is incorporated in the pages of this *Dictionary* and *Miscellany*.

Clarke was aware of the degree to which England lagged behind the Continent in these studies, and of the gaps in the then state of knowledge of various branches of bibliography. In his §2 of the second volume of the *Miscellany*, which is devoted to the history of printing, Clarke pleads for an analysis of the 'characters' (i.e. the types) of undated editions. 'If this were made systematically, how much light might it be expected to afford us in clearing up the first epochs of our typographical hiſtory.' He then adds that 'the excellent work of P. Placidus Braun may serve as a model'.

Clarke was a remarkable man to whom we owe the firſt methodical and inſtruƈted attempt to codify bibliographical knowledge as it had been accumulated and syſtematized in Italy, France and Germany. He was the firſt English writer to view bibliography as a science. To him, also, we owe the preference in English of the gallicisms 'bibliography' and 'bibliographer' over 'bibliology' and 'bibliologer', which may be found in contemporary use. Egerton Brydges's *The British Bibliographer*, a series of articles on the work of British dramatiſts, essayiſts, etc., appeared in 1810–14 (four volumes). Thereafter bibliography was firmly eſtablished, though its meaning may have remained imprecise. It was, however, diſtinƈt from bibliophily and the bibliomania (also gallicisms) which were popularized by the Rev. Thomas Frognall Dibdin (1776–1847) who firſt began writing on bibliographical subjeƈts in Clarke's time. Dibdin's *Introduƈtion to the Knowledge of rare and valuable editions of the Greek and Latin Classics* was published in 1802.

THOMAS FROGNALL DIBDIN, 1810–19,
AND THOMAS HARTWELL HORNE, 1818–21

While Napoleon was extending his conqueſts (and, incidentally, abſtraƈting the exotic founts from the Vatican and depositing them in the French National Printing Office), Dibdin was editing Herbert's expansion of Ames's *Typographical Antiquities*. The volumes were published between 1810 and 1819. Also, Dibdin, who properly appreciated the riches of the library of the third Earl Spencer, founded the Roxburghe Club in 1812, and published the *Bibliotheca Spenceriana* in 1814–15. When Europe settled down after 1815, Dibdin went on a book-buying tour. Dibdin's *Bibliographical Decameron* (1817) in three volumes is the moſt sumptuous and elaborate monument of his enthuſiaſtic explorations into typographical antiquity. His *Reminiscences of a Literary Life* (two volumes) were published in 1836.

A less spectacular but in some respects more utilitarian writer than Dibdin was his contemporary, Horne. The Rev. Thomas Hartwell Horne (1780–1862), who liked to describe himself as 'Presbyter of the Reformed Protestant Episcopal Church of England and Ireland', was rector of St Nicholas Acons and Christchurch, Newgate, before he went to the British Museum in 1824 (where he stayed until 1860). He held the position of senior assistant in the Printed Books Department, where he was prominent in the design and arrangement of the new general catalogue. When not thundering against popery and campaigning against tractarianism, Horne consecrated his time to biblical studies, and for their sake devoted himself to the discipline of bibliography. His *Introduction to the Critical Study and Knowledge of the Holy Scriptures* (London, 1818–21), of which several editions were published, is remembered; while his *Introduction to the Study of Bibliography* (London, 1814, two volumes) is forgotten, though it was a notable book in its time and, like the man himself, deserving of recognition in any account of the progress of our study.

Horne's *Introduction to Bibliography* owes its substance and system immediately to Clarke's *Bibliographical Dictionary* ('Indispensable', says Horne), and through him to De Bure (the method of whose *Bibliographie Instructive* he greatly admired), Cailleau's *Dictionnaire bibliographique* (to which he makes acknowledgement), Peignot (whose *Répertoire bibliographique* is much quoted); much of his detail to Brunet's *Manuel* and his taste to Dibdin (whose *Bibliographical Decameron* he esteemed).

Unlike Clarke, who only liked a few large-paper copies of his book, Horne was also a bibliophile and gratefully mentions Baskerville, though not Bell. The work of Bensley and Bulmer 'may justly be ranked among the finest specimens of typography. The letter-press of Macklin's splendid edition of the Bible, and of Bowyer's magnificent edition of Hume, by Mr Bensley, and the superb Shakespeare, Milton, and other works by Mr Bulmer, will justly vie with the most costly productions of Bodoni' (1, pp. 253–4). Horne's *Introduction* is a good, if not a 'fine' piece of printing. A large-paper copy is undoubtedly a desirable possession. The illuſtrative woodcuts and engravings are fine and were from the hand of J. Lee, the well-known craftsman comparable with Richard Auſtin.

Horne provides a ſeĉtion on the 'Mechanism of Printing' which comprises a description of the types used. He gives the sizes then current (from French Canon down to Diamond) and shows specimens intended 'to convey a correĉt idea of their various sizes' and, the author might have added, 'designs'. He does not otherwise describe the types which, as to the large bodies, are the new 'fat faces' cut by Robert Thorne, and the smaller perhaps by William Miller, and others by Vincent Figgins, which were in the office of Horne's printer, George Woodfall.

An intereſting faĉt is that, while the Horne-Woodfall founts are 'modern face', as a specimen they are inferior in arrangement to those shown in the trade manuals such as Luckombe's *Concise Hiſtory of the Origin and Progress of Printing* (London, 1771) which shows the 'old faces' of Caslon, Fry and Cottrell. Fry's founts are again shown in C. Stower's second edition of John Smith's *Printer's Grammar* and in the third edition of 1808. Woodfall was an excellent printer, but he did not encourage Horne to ſtudy typographical variations and he remained, in this respeĉt, inferior to Clarke who, it has been seen, was well aware of the importance of ſtudying them. The virtues of Horne's *Introduĉtion*, considerable as they are, advanced the ſtudy of typography only in its literary and antiquarian aspeĉts. A similar judgement muſt be passed upon the work of a greater contemporary bibliographer. In terms of the observation of typographical variation and classification, Dibdin and Horne had progressed no farther than to divide types into the categories of Black-Letter, Roman and Italic.

It has been remarked that Clarke had seen the point of Braun's scientific typographical analysis. Dibdin, on the other hand, was ruled by taſte and antiquarian zeal. He was the leader of the late eighteenth-century English school of 'bibliomania', which loved the ancient, the rare, the curious and the sumptuous in printed books. He was the ideal inspirer and supporter of the rich and noble 'large paper' colle&or. The Roxburghe Club, named in honour of the third Duke, which he had brought into exi&ence under his own presidency, had done much for the e&ablishment of a ta&e, among men of wealth and title, for manuscripts equally with printed books. The Club's publications, &ill in progress, of fine and sumptuous facsimiles, edited by the members themselves or by scholars, ju&ifies abundant gratitude to Dibdin. The mo& famous bibliophile of his age was 71 when he died in 1847.

THE FOUNDER OF MODERN SCIENTIFIC BIBLIOGRAPHY, WILLIAM BLADES, LONDON, 1861

In the year of Dibdin's death there came out of his apprenticeship, at the age of 23, the ma&er printer to whom Europe owes the foundation of the modern English school of scientific bibliography. William Blades was born at Clapham in 1824, and, after attending the local grammar school, was apprenticed at the age of 16 to his father's printing office in Abchurch Lane, London. The fir& volume of his *Life and Typography of William Caxton* (London, 1861) completely revolutionized the attitude of scholars everywhere towards early printing.

With the exceptions of Laire and Panzer, librarians and scholars, when examining the authenticity of a given book, relied wholly upon a general impression gained from the handling of it. Any que&ion of the place of printing of a given book, or its date, was settled empirically by the general impression and 'feeling' thus aroused. Nothing more, indeed, was possible until Blades began.

'Ames, Herbert, Lowndes and Dr Dibdin (England's representative bibliographer) were quite unable to di&inguish between different but similar types.' So said Blades. He e&ablished entirely new &andards of accuracy by sub&ituting for the 'general impression' or a 'feeling', the degree of proof that was set up by tireless inspe&ion of every piece of printing that was ascribable (in his case) to Caxton. The minute examination of the types of a given book included the manner in which the words, lines and paragraphs were composed, also the style in which the pages were made up, signed and printed. Blades conducted his investigation on the theory that every ancient printed book differed from copy to copy so much that each had its 'individuality'. His theory and practice were absolutely new and, as time has proved, so justified that they have been accepted by all incunabulists of all countries.

Blades's predecessors in point of method were Laire and Braun. The near-certainty is that Blades's method, so much more elaborate than Braun's, was independently devised. These are the reasons. First, the insights gained by an experienced master, as Blades now was, gave him a distinct advantage in any detailed typographical investigation over any man detached from the trade. Secondly, Blades possessed a technical knowledge of the means of reproduction not available to Laire and Braun. This meant that, in his capacity as author, he could call upon himself, as printer, to provide an infinitely (the word is not too strong) more subtle means of reproduction than those available to earlier scholars.

'Being familiar with all branches of the Art, I have endeavoured to use my practical experience in assisting me to discover the materials and practices employed while the Press was yet in its infancy' (p. vii of the Preface to volume 1). So wrote Blades with type and composition in mind. His attitude towards the means of reproduction was not less exhaustive. He records in more than one paragraph his gratitude to one Tupper, master of the art of reproduction invented by Aloysius Sene-felder (1771–1834). Lithography was the process that made possible the visible demonstration of Blades's thesis. This was absolutely new in 1861 (the year, by the way, in which the word 'incunable' came into the English language), when the first volume on the life of Caxton was published by Blades at the age of 37. It was supremely fortunate for bibliography, in the broadest sense, that such a range of enviable means to the accomplishment of an original typographical investigation should have been matched, as it was in Blades, by the rarely found, but necessary faculties of perception, deduction and scrupulosity.

Blades's second volume on the typography of Caxton was published in 1863. The author was aware that he was an innovator. 'The Reader's attention is drawn to several particulars hitherto unrecorded, such as a complete synopsis of every fount of letter used by Caxton, with an Alphabet of each, including all the single, double, and triple letters, signs, contractions, etc. – the chronological sequence traceable in the various founts of letter'; so writes Blades on p. v of the Introduction to his second volume. He there lays down the proposition that 'Minute typographical research is by no means a matter of idle or trivial curiosity'. The work, which occupied years, was inevitably that of an autodidact. Nevertheless, Blades had attracted an academic friend whose assistance he highly valued and thus acknowledged: 'To H. Bradshaw Esq., of King's College, Cambridge, I owe much for information concerning the true collation of the early unsigned books, as well as for numerous suggestions and critical remarks while many sheets were passing through the Press.' It was through Bradshaw that bibliography, as Blades understood and practised it, began to be an academic 'subject'.

BLADES'S INFLUENCE ON
HENRY BRADSHAW OF CAMBRIDGE

Blades began his acquaintance with Bradshaw in 1857, when both were ardent students of Caxton. Bradshaw's incapacity to organize his correspondence made systematic collaboration impossible, but the two exchanged letters over a period of twenty-five years; and from it there developed the method which, in due time, became the basis of modern typographical investigation whether into fifteenth-century or into later problems. Bradshaw piled additions and corrections on to Blades's pages but was equally generous with appreciation. 'The fact is', he wrote to Blades, 'that it is only by having your book constantly before me that I am able to work out any of the many things which are now becoming daily clearer to me.'

The connexion with Bradshaw led to a wider acceptance of Blades's principle that 'minute typographical research' was the reverse of being the equivalent of 'idle and trivial curiosity'. Moreover, it was not sufficient to colleƈt the obvious conſtituent alphabetical and other symbols. Blades needed to know whether those typographical conſtituents were identical throughout the composition in which they were used; or whether, in the course of produƈtion, it became necessary to redesign, recut or repair certain sorts. Hence, he compared all the appearances of all the sorts on all the pages and so traced all their varieties of 'ſtate'. Such was Blades's idea of thoroughness as applied to a book of the fifteenth century. In later life Blades extended his intereſt beyond the fifteenth century to the progress of printing thenceforward. The ſtudy is necessarily bound up with the hiſtory, material and produƈtion of six inſtitutions: the House of Plantin at Antwerp, the Luther Foundry at Frankfurt am Main, the Stamperia Vaticana at Rome, the University Press at Oxford, the House of Enschedé at Haarlem and the Imprimerie Royale at Paris. Much of the work done by scholars on these printing houses owes its inspiration, direƈtly or otherwise, to Blades.

BLADES'S INFLUENCE ABROAD

The work of C. Ruelens and A. De Backer, *Annales Plantiniennes depuis la Fondation de l'Imprimerie plantinienne à Anvers jusqu'à la mort de Chr. Plantin (1555–1589)*, published at Brussels in 1865, is the firſt modern hiſtorical account of the moſt famous of all the houses of sixteenth-century foundation.

Of great significance in Blades's development of intereſt in poſt-fifteenth-century ſtudies was the *Specimen de Caraƈtères Typographiques de Joh. Enschedé et Fils. Imprimeurs à Haarlem* (Haarlem, 1867). The moſt hiſtoric of all foundries had at its head one competent to a greater degree, in many respeƈts, than Erneſti or Fournier to assess the importance of the ancient punches and matrices in his firm's possession – at the apex of which ſtands the fount of Henric 'de lettersnider'

(1490–1518). Blades reviewed the book and later showed his appreciation of the subject by listing all the typefounders' specimens that he had collected. This was the first time since Lottin that such a list had been prepared. Blades had now, by 1875 and at the age of fifty or so, turned to the sixteenth century. The St Bride copy of A.J. Enschedé's *Specimen* is annotated by Blades with the names of Van Dijk, Fleischman and Rosart, as the engravers of their respective letters. Blades also translated and transcribed the introduction by Ioannes Enschedé (the first of the line) to the firm's *Specimen* of 1768. This, at its period, was inevitably a eulogy of Fleischman, while Van Dijk hardly gets mention. That such books as Enschedé's *Specimen* of 1867 and the century-earlier one of 1768 were given so detailed a study by Blades is one more proof of his thoroughness.

The first librarian to adopt the method of Blades was J. W. Holtrop, who, having catalogued in 1856 the fifteenth-century books in the Royal Library at The Hague, published, five years after the second volume of Blades's Caxton, a very considerable work, *Monuments Typographiques des Pays-Bas au quinzième siècle.* Bradshaw acknowledged himself to be Holtrop's pupil. It must be remembered that, after his Caxton, Blades never looked back to the fifteenth century. As a practical printer he never became a 'dedicated' incunabulist. In 1868 his pupil in the general study of fifteenth-century printing published his first essay in the bibliography of incunabula. He modestly called it a 'memorandum' on the output of the anonymous Cologne printer of the *Historia Sancti Albani.* Later he printed a second memorandum entitled *A Classified Index of the fifteenth Century Books in the Collection of M. J. De Meyer,* then being offered for sale by auction at Ghent. The Ghent Catalogue was an important piece. Hitherto nothing of the kind had been seen. 'The auction catalogues issued by the first houses in England and France are a standing disgrace to the two countries so far as this class of books is concerned', says Bradshaw at p. 3 of his *Index* (London, Macmillan and Co., Price one shilling [then]).

The collection was for sale at Ghent, and Bradshaw, provided with £100 by the Cambridge Library Syndicate, went to the sale. As he spent double the sum he felt justified in lavishing huge labour on his *Index*. Having described the conventional method of classifying incunabula under countries, towns and presses, he argues that these details need supplementing. An important progressive step in method is Bradshaw's consistent reference to existing facsimiles and his indication, in Blades's style, of the types used in the books of a specific printer. He gives his reasons at pp. 15–16. What he was striving for was 'such an accurate and methodical study of the types used and habits of printing observable at different presses, as to enable him [the bibliographer] to observe and be guided by these characteristics in settling the date of a book which bears no date on the surface . . . We desire that the types and habits of each printer should be made a special subject of study . . . In fact each press must be looked upon as a *genus* and each book as a *species* . . . The study of palaeotypography has been hitherto mainly such a *dilettante* matter, that people have shrunk from going into such details, though when once studied as a branch of natural history, it is as fruitful in interesting results as most subjects.'

Once more it may be said that this application of what Bradshaw calls, in a cumbrous Linnaeanism, the 'natural history method', however elementary it may seem to us, was then a novelty. 'Except', says Bradshaw in his shilling pamphlet (p. 16), 'Mr Blades's monograph of Caxton's press, The Hague *Catalogus* and [Holtrop's] *Monuments Typographiques* are the only books existing in any literature, so far as I know, which render the study of palaeotypography in any way possible upon a proper basis.' Bradshaw is correct: these works represent the beginning of scientific, comparative typography; and what we would nowadays describe as modern 'bibliography'; that is to say, they represent the first steps towards the complex analysis of book-production which is best exemplified in contemporary writing by Messrs Carter and Pollard's *Enquiry into the Nature of certain Nineteenth Century Pamphlets* (London, 1934). In Blades's and Bradshaw's day, specialist students of manuscripts and printed books had not acquired an organization of their own. They pursued their subject side by side with professional librarians, but did not, apparently, sit down together.

A notable event is reported in the Library Association's periodical for December 1891 when Blades and others resolved to found a new association to be called The Bibliographical Society.

Palaeotypography, or the comparative study of typography, then got its chance to establish itself as a study necessary to those professionally concerned with books printed in the fifteenth century and since. Within ten years of the foundation of the Society the scientific knowledge of books printed between ?1440 and 1520 in the European countries was subjected to a novel impulse. Implicitly, the accurate classification of early printed books was now to be undertaken. An influence far more powerful for what is now called bibliography than that of the Roxburghe Club, or the Library Association, was now initiated.

BLADES AND THE CAXTON EXHIBITION, LONDON, 1877

An international event created a new interest among bibliophiles, librarians and bibliographers – and stimulated the curiosity of the general public: a comprehensive exhibition organized by the printing trade. Towards the end of the year 1874 the Secretary of the Printers' Pension Corporation, Mr J. S. Hodson, wishing to benefit the pensioners, decided to celebrate the appearance in Westminster in 1474, according to common knowledge, of the first book to be printed in this country: *The Game and Play of Chesse*. Among those who received the announcements circulated to all master-printers was the head of the firm of Blades, East and Blades. The Secretary found himself in correspondence with a master-printer who did not believe that the *Chesse* book was printed (1) at Westminster, (2) by Caxton, or (3) in 1474. What Blades had already proved was far from being general knowledge; it had not got into the encyclopaedias, nor into the history books. According to Blades, Caxton was not established in England as a printer until 1476; his first book printed here was the *Dictes and Sayenges of the philosophers*, finished at Westminster in 1477, and so dated. The *Dictes*, accordingly, ranks as the first dated book printed in England, though it is believed that others preceded it.

The moral of this story is that Blades's conviction that the date given as '1477' was authentic did not arise from the general impression left in the mind of an experienced collector, but from patient typographic analysis. That is to say, Blades compared all the types used for the composition of all the books connected with Caxton, whether in Cologne (where he became acquainted with the art), Bruges (where he had the assistance of Colard Mansion), and Westminster (where he was in business on his sole account). The Caxton Exhibition was postponed to 1877 and Blades dominated it. The Exhibition was conceived in no insular spirit. It was a supreme visual embodiment of what the great international art had done and was doing internationally. Nor was it only an antiquarian Exhibition. Its initiatives having come from the trade, the organizing committee, naturally, bore the names of well-known printers. As Blades acted as the general manager, the whole enterprise was executed with unusual thoroughness, as may be seen from the Catalogue, which was edited by George Bullen, Keeper of the Printed Books, British Museum. The collaboration of members of the printing trade with officials of the British Museum and the principal librarians resulted in one of the most beneficial if least conspicuous advantages of the Exhibition.

The curators of collections, no less than members of the public, were given the opportunity to familiarize themselves with the development of the art; its great monuments in terms of the Bible, the Liturgy, Literature and Illustration. However excellent and comprehensive the antiquarian side, the contemporary state of the art was no less well considered. Hand-presses, machine-presses, copperplate-presses; modern stereotyping and electrotyping appliances – and many other practical elements in the contemporary composing and press rooms were shown and described. Notable among the educational exhibits was a rich collection of books relating to the history and practice of printing, lent and commented upon by Blades; to which was added a remarkable assemblage of typefounding materials: punches, matrices, moulds, casting-machines, etc.

Among the sources of antiquities, Oxford lent 'punchions' and matrices from Dr Fell's colleƈtion; Messrs Caslon lent original punches cut
by William Caslon I; Messrs Reed lent the matrices of an English Black-
Letter formerly Wolfe's, *c.* 1581. More relevant to this sketch was a
magnificent colleƈtion of typefounder's Specimen Books, the firﬅ ever
to be publicly shown. The catalogue, with an introduƈtion, was compiled by a new recruit to bibliography and comparative typography:
Talbot Baines Reed, then 25 years of age.

TALBOT BAINES REED AND THE FIRST
SCIENTIFIC HISTORY OF TYPEFOUNDING

Reed was born in London in 1852, the third son of Sir Charles Reed,
M.P. for Hackney, who owned the Fann Street typefoundry. Young
Reed entered the foundry in 1869. But for the Caxton Exhibition of
1877 he might never have ﬅepped aside from writing articles on sports,
games and open-air subjeƈts; but for Blades he might never have de-
serted the *Boy's Own Paper*, to whose volume 1, no. 1, he contributed.
Reed's success with *The Fifth Form at St Dominic's* (1887) might well
have led him away from the printing trade. But the inspiration of
Blades's example and an innate sense of dignity decided Reed, in the
intervals of writing school ﬅories, to persevere with the hiﬅory of
typefounding. From 1877 a new spirit informed English effort. The
Exhibition, though dedicated to Caxton, had not been limited by na-
tionaliﬅ prejudice. Its catalogue was handsomely printed (in old-ﬅyle
type) at the Elzevir Press (a short-lived house begun by W. H. Wilkins,
formerly of the Chiswick Press), and its effeƈt was felt abroad.

In 1880 Alphonse Willems published a subﬅantial volume. *Les
Elʒevier: hiﬅoire et annales typographiques* championed the theory that
Van Dijk was responsible for the typographical material of the Elzevirs. In 1882 Max Rooses published his folio *Chriﬅophe Plantin, imprimeur anversois*, which is the firﬅ modern biographical survey of the
printer's religious, political and cultural relations. Five years later Eng-

land produced a massive, original but by no means spectacular publication. The work, a quarto, had been stimulated by the Caxton Exhibition, and the example of Blades, whom the author of the work had first met during the course of its preparation. Talbot Baines Reed's *History of the Old English Letter Foundries* came from the house of Elliot Stock (a publisher who specialized in antiquarian literature) in 1887. The contents go far beyond their title and provide a rich fund of general information never before collected on foreign foundries, their types and the printers who used them. Its author contrived an unprecedented wealth of typographical illustration and documented the whole in a degree only attainable by himself.

In 1890 Reed lectured to the Royal Society of Arts on 'Old and New Fashions in Typography'. The lecture is important, especially in our case, because it comprises the first exposition and discussion in English of the origins and purposes of Louis XIV's scientific commission on the typographical alphabet and its rationalist results as rendered in the geometrical patterns that served for the Romain du Roi of Louis XIV. Reed's lecture was delivered on 16 April 1890. He was then 38 years of age. It was a memorable occasion. In the audience was Emery Walker. The text (printed without the aid of the illustrations that, in the form of lantern slides, elucidated his words) appeared later in the Society's transactions. Unfortunately it has never since been separately published and is virtually unknown. At one time Updike, recognizing its significance while knowing that at a few points it needed correction, considered editing and reprinting the text. Owing to the war, the project was abandoned and typographical literature thus deprived of a valuable addition.

REED'S APPRECIATION OF THE
DOCUMENTARY VALUE OF TYPE SPECIMENS

One of Reed's great advantages was that, as a trade typefounder, he had studied typefounders' specimens with practical insight aided by

wide reading. His 'Li&t of the Principal Authorities Consulted' comprised 150 items and there is every reason to credit him with having
read them. He had the books in his personal possession or on loan from
Blades. His words about his preceptor are worth reprinting since they
do not appear in the edition of 1952.

'My foremo&t thanks are due to my honoured and valued friend, Mr
William Blades, to whom I am indebted for far more than unlimited access to his valuable typographical library, and the ungrudging use of
his special knowledge on all subje&ts conne&ted with English typography. These I have enjoyed, and what was of equal value his kindly advice and sympathy during the whole progress of a work which, but for
his encouragement from the outset, might never have been completed.'

Next Reed thanked Henry Bradshaw for his intere&t in the book,
which he 'enriched by more than one valuable communication'.

It has been seen already that the &tudy of the specimens issued by
the typefounders as documents had fir&t been appreciated by Blades
who published what Rowe Mores would have called a 'Dissertation' on
that subje&t in 1875; also that this 'Dissertation' by Blades and the specimen sheets and books that he had been the fir&t to colle&t were fir&t
made the basis of a consecutive hi&tory of the English trade by Reed.

This was a bibliographical lesson that Reed never forgot. As a typefounder himself, he exaggerated when he argued that 'A Colle&tion of
Typefounder's Specimen Books arranged chronologically will, perhaps, furnish a more useful hi&tory of the art than any that could be written'. Reed himself had already proved the importance of typefounders'
specimens in his *magnum opus*, 'the imperfe&tions of which', Reed says,
'are apparent to no one as painfully as they are to the writer'. This &tate-
ment, even when limited by 'perhaps', is far too mode&t an e&timate of
his powers of dige&tion and exposition, not to mention reading and research. Reed's book either in its fir&t edition of 1887 or even when so
worthily edited and generously supplemented as in its second edition of
1952, given us by Mr A. F. Johnson, does not supersede the &tudy of the
Specimens. His book makes the Specimens more, not less, significant.

In the truest sense, the Specimen Books become more important as more comment is bestowed upon them. The span of the illustrative material that Reed gives is ample, but it is less than adequate because it is selective. Even then a comprehensive collection of typefounders' Specimen Books is far from being within the possibilities open even to Blades and Reed; nor is access to a public collection of this kind convenient outside London. That the metropolis is peculiarly fortunate in this regard is due to the specialized collections formed by Blades the printer and Reed the typefounder and now kept at St Bride's in London. The debt which the study, now pursued internationally, owes to Blades and Reed is incalculable.

TYPOGRAPHICAL STUDIES
AFTER BLADES'S DEATH, 1890

In 1890 Blades died, in his sixty-sixth year, having accomplished a bibliographical task which for originality and mass surpassed all precedent. His teaching and example were not ineffectual. Principal among those who, early, felt his influence were Bradshaw and next Reed. A follower of Blades at one remove was Edward Gordon Duff, who was inspired by Bradshaw, to whose memory he dedicated his *Early Printed Books* (1893). At Cambridge, Henry Bradshaw's successor, Francis Jenkinson, maintained Blades's doctrine and expounded his method. Duff, as one of his circle, was the inspirer of others, the most significant of whom was Robert Proctor, who became England's – and, it is not too much to say, the world's – foremost incunabulist. The scientific study of fifteenth-century books made continued progress in the nineties.

In 1891, exactly thirty years after the publication of Blades's first volume on Caxton, a new edition of the *Repertorium Bibliographicum* of Ludwig Hain, the Munich librarian, appeared. Beginning in 1826, it was left at his death in 1836 indexed only under printers. These summary indexes were completely redigested and vastly expanded in 1891 by Konrad Burger. The comparative study of typography greatly profited from Burger's provision of a chronological list of books arranged under their respective printers, with the undated books arranged alphabetically. The new index enabled the reader to estimate at a glance the known output of any fifteenth-century press.

Like palaeography, our study benefited to an incalculable degree from the popularization of photographic means of reproduction. It is obvious from Blades's threefold mention of one Tupper, his lithographer, that the printing of the documentary illustrations to the Caxton in 1861 was no easy matter even to a master-printer. The production of facsimiles on a national basis was begun by J. W. Holtrop whose *Monuments typographiques des Pays-Bas* (1868) is mentioned above. The use of facsimiles was given a strong impulse when Thièrry-Poux's *Premiers monuments de l'imprimerie en France au XVᵉ siècle* was published in 1890. In 1892 Burger initiated his *Monumenta Germaniae et Italiae Typographica*, the first modern set of facsimiles and pages of fifteenth-century books collected on an international basis. In England the Typefacsimile Society, founded in 1900 and working until 1909, forwarded the study. Meanwhile, too, the Germans were preparing to undertake the difficult work of identifying all the productions of the first German and Italian presses. To accomplish this more facsimiles were necessary and the Gesellschaft für Typenkunde des XV. Jahrhunderts was founded in 1907.

THE BRITISH MUSEUM CATALOGUE OF FIFTEENTH-
CENTURY BOOKS, LONDON, 1908, IN PROGRESS

At home, the work of E. Gordon Duff represents a concrete extension of Blades's method to our prototypographers after Caxton.

Duff was an Oxford man whose first writing on bibliography was a contribution to the first volume of the Oxford Historical Society's *Collectanea* published in 1885. Next year he began cataloguing the Bodleian incunabula and at about this time, according to A. W. Pollard, he heard of the tastes and talents of Robert Proctor. Duff invited him

and some Oxford friends to dine when, says A. W. Pollard, he 'expounded bibliography to a doubtless devoutly impressed audience. To
Proétor, who was anxious to take up some definite piece of bibliographical work, he suggeſted the Press of John of Doesbrough, the
Antwerp printer.' Duff's catalogue of the Bodleian incunabula was
continued by Proétor. Meanwhile, he published his firſt work, *Early
Printed Books* (in Kegan Paul's series edited by A. W. Pollard) and dedicated it 'to the Memory of Henry Bradshaw', whom, says H.F. Stewart, 'he never saw and only wrote to once, having arrived at the sound
method [of bibliography] by an independent path and being confirmed
therein by his friend and successor, Francis Jenkinson' (whose biogra-
phy was written by Stewart), a learned incunabuliſt.

    In the year of publication of Duff's *Early Printed Books* (London,
1893), 'the young Napoleon of Bibliography' as MacAliſter called him,
was appointed Librarian at the Rylands Library, Mancheſter, where he
remained until 1900. While he was there Proétor's monograph on John
of Doesbrough, dedicated to Duff, was published (1894) by the Bibliographical Society. Proétor acknowledged in his Preface that 'for never
failing help, advice, and encouragement I am deeply indebted to Mr
Edward Gordon Duff'.

    While it is true that Duff arrived at the 'sound' method by an inde-
pendent path, 'that is, independent from Bradshaw', he adopted, in
explicit terms, Bradshaw's 'natural hiſtory' view of typographical classification. A Press was a genus, a book was a species. This is Blades's
method, though not his nomenclature. And Duff had proper reſpeét for
Blades. His *Caxton* and Edmond's *Aberdeen Printers* 'are the beſt
monographs we possess', Duff says in *Early English Printing*. It should
be added that he later argued that Blades's analysis of Caxton's types
by form, irreſpeétive of chronology, had the disadvantage of misleading
tyros. The development of scientific terminology was not rapid during
the period. Duff's intereſts ceased to be general. He specialized on
English typographical hiſtory 1476–1557, and perhaps recognized the
superiority of Proétor's authentic visual memory for typographical

variation. Duff's *Early English Printing* (1896) provides facsimiles of all English fifteenth-century types, lists and numbers them, but does not describe or name them. Proctor's *Tracts on Early Printing* (1895, dedicated to Francis Jenkinson 'with respect and gratitude') includes a list of the founts of type and woodcut devices used by the printers of the Southern Netherlands in the fifteenth century. This, the author says, is 'a humble attempt to complete in some sort the work of Mr Bradshaw . . .'.

In 1898 a work of the first importance appeared. Whereas the lists of fifteenth-century books drawn up by Panzer in his *Annales Typographici* group the books in alphabetical sequence of printing centres, and Hain's *Repertorium bibliographicum* arranged the books under the names of the authors, and Burger's Index (1891) arranged the printers in alphabetical order, Robert Proctor's *Index to the Early Printed Books in the British Museum*, while also arranging the books under their printers, ordered them chronologically under the towns in which they worked. This gave practical effect to a plan that Bradshaw had intended in 1870. When Proctor realized it in 1898 it was a magnificent contribution to the study. Proctor enumerated and described all the types known to be used by each printer. Seven years later Konrad Haebler expanded Proctor's typographical enumeration with his *Typenrepertorium der Wiegendrucke*. This came out in 1905. At last it became possible, on typographical grounds, to assign books without imprints, whether originating in Germany or elsewhere, to their probable printers. The British Museum had by now decided to undertake its *Catalogue of Books Printed in the Fifteenth Century*, of which the first volume was published in 1908 and the eighth in 1949.

The British Museum Catalogue represents the highest and broadest application of the Blades-Proctor-Haebler method. Besides making, incidentally, a generous contribution to the statistical and geographical criticism of fifteenth-century theological and literary, liturgical and legal production the Catalogue is essentially the classic example of palaeo-typographical method applied to books printed before 1501. There is no need to pursue the point farther than to say that Blades's method first exemplified in respeƈt of one English printer in the fifteenth century in 1861, reached its full development in the Catalogue begun in 1908 which is planned to cover the produƈtion of printers in all countries. Its acceptance by scholars, foreign and native, dispenses the present sketch from any further hiſtory of the origin and evolution of what may well be called the Blades-Proƈtor-Haebler syſtem of classifying incunabula, measuring the bodies of the types in which they were composed and grouping them according to major diſtinƈtions in design.

The method was adversely criticized by Ernſt Consentius who opposed its adoption by the German (Weimar) Government's Commission set up to compile a new, general and complete Catalogue of incunables preserved in the libraries of the world. The plans for this projeƈt had been laid in 1904 and an inventory of the books in German libraries completed in 1911. The war and its entailments delayed the work and the firſt volume was not out until 1925. Consentius pressed his arguments from 1929. They were countered by Haebler in 1932 and Wehmer in 1933. Work on the *Gesamtkatalog* proceeded in accordance with the Blades-Proƈtor-Haebler method.

REED AS BLADES'S SUCCESSOR; HIS DEATH IN 1893

From this point the present sketch concerns itself with the methodical criticisms of poſt-incunabular typography. As has been seen, Blades initiated academic librarians into praƈtical typography through the medium of his *Caxton* and his domination of the Caxton Exhibition. The public display of the materials and methods involved in the praƈtice of the art and myſtery of typography completed the transformation of eighteenth-century bibliophily into nineteenth-century bibliography. The difference between Herbert and Dibdin on the one hand and Blades and Proƈtor on the other was profound. The former were produƈts of an age of ariſtocratic taſte and connoisseurship and the latter of an age of middle-class efficiency and science. Blades was an eminent representative of the middle class. In 1891 Reed completed

Blades's poſthumous *Pentateuch of Printing* with a memoir of the author and a liſt of his works. Reed, another middle-class man, was now
the driving force in bibliography. He was always ready to leɕture, even
in the provinces. He was also aɕtive as Hon. Secretary of the Bibliographical Society. In 1891 he delivered before the Library Association
a paper 'On the Use and Classification of a Typographical Library'
(which was printed in *The Library*, vol. IV (London, 1893), pp. 33–44).
Reed repeated his argument that a colleɕtion of typefounders' specimens, arranged chronologically, would be a more useful hiſtory of the
art than any book. Meanwhile he was at work on school ſtories. His
'maſterpiece' in this line, *The Fifth Form at St Dominic's*, his firſt true
school ſtory, came out in 1887. *Tom, Dick and Harry* was published in
1892. With *The Cock-House at Fellsgarth* on his hands in 1891 as well as
the family typefoundry business of Sir Charles Reed and Sons, of
which he was managing direɕtor, an energetic member of the Highgate
Congregational Church, a Fellow of the Society of Antiquaries and a
member of the Reform and Savile Clubs, Reed was not short of oppor-
tunities of employment and recreation.

By this time Reed's health was failing. The author of the *Hiſtory of
the Old English Letter Foundries*, his greateſt book by which he is leaſt
known, died at Highgate on 29 November 1893. The deaths of Blades
in 1890 and Reed in 1893 deprived the trade and bibliography of their
two moſt learned and praɕtical teachers. Who among printers or typefounders, at home or abroad, would fill their place?

Three years after Reed's death another erudite and praɕtical typefounder made his initial appearance in print, Charles Enschedé. His firſt
dissertation began with what was, in part, a rejeɕtion of Willems's thesis
that the Elzevir types originated with Van Dijk in Amſterdam. According to Enschedé, the types (or matrices thereof), whose origin was in
queſtion, came from the Egenelff-Berner-Luther foundry at Frankfurt.
He based his argument, however, on the identity of the Greeks in the
Elzevir *Specimen* of 1658 and the Luther *Specimen* of 1718. But the dates
were too late to carry the weight of Enschedé's counter-thesis and con-

sequently the queſtion of their origin remained in suspense. No scholar in or out of the printing trade could then carry the subjeƈt farther.

WILLIAM MORRIS AND EMERY WALKER, 1892

Meanwhile, an event of great potency occurred. In 1888 the newly founded Arts and Crafts Exhibition Society, an offshoot of the Art Workers Guild formed in 1884, arranged its firſt public demonſtration of the decoration of utilities, among which 'fine' printing was given its place. With William Morris among the founders was Emery Walker, a trade printer and engraver who was endowed also with a sense of ſtyle and had acquired a knowledge of incunables. The catalogue of the Exhibition embodied the text of a leƈture on printing by Walker. The whole enterprise gave an impetus, ſtill ſtrong, to the praƈtice of calligraphy and typography as decorative arts. Morris and Walker inaugurated an era of taſte and colleƈting more laſting and widespread than that of Dibdin and created generations of British and foreign admirers of manuscripts and early printed books. It created an intereſt in lettering, whether written or printed, that was intelligent as well as enthusiaſtic, for it was based upon a solid underſtanding of the forms, development and hiſtory of scripts and types.

After Morris's firſt modeſt experiments with the Chiswick Press and next with his speƈtacular achievements at the Kelmscott Press from 1891, there began a new period of aeſthetic appreciation of letter-design far more discriminating than was possible in the older period of Dibdin. The principal gain from the Kelmscott Chaucer was less its challenge to half a century of exploitation which notwithſtanding the example of the Chiswick and other Presses, and that of some houses associated with the Oxford Movement, had reduced the mass of printing almoſt to the level of one of the loweſt aspeƈts of ruthless induſtrialism; nor its championship of the ſtandards of the medieval manuscript and the later incunable; nor Morris's onslaught on the 'sweltering hideousness of Bodoni' with his pinched romans and wry italics. The impor-

tant faĉt was that printing henceforth became once more intimately associated with literature and art – as it had been when Louis XIV
charged the Academic Commission with responsibility for designating
a new roman, and ultimately produced the volume of *Médailles* in 1702
which was, in its way, as speĉtacular an achievement as the Kelmscott
Chaucer in 1896.

The end of the nineteenth century witnessed a notable advance in
English ﬆudy of modern hiﬆory. In 1895 Aĉton, at the age of sixty-one,
was appointed Regius Professor of Modern Hiﬆory at Cambridge in
succession to Seeley, who had held the Chair for a quarter of a century.
Aĉton's inaugural leĉture, delivered at Cambridge in June 1895, emphasized the importance of the change that occurred in the middle of the
century with the opening of new archives and the ﬆudy of documents.
Yet, with new documents in hand 'it is by solidity of criticism more than
by the plenitude of erudition, that the ﬆudy of hiﬆory ﬆrengthens and
ﬆraightens and extends the mind'. By criticism Aĉton meant the ascer-
tainment of the value of the document in terms of its authorship, its
transcription and its integrity. Hence, for Aĉton, the critical eﬆimate of
an accepted authority was even more important than the discovery of a
new document. Notwithﬆanding, 'Hiﬆory, to be above evasion or dis-
pute, muﬆ ﬆand on documents, not on opinions'. It was a diĉtum that
fell gracefully upon the ears of those who had learnt from Blades, Bradshaw and Jenkinson at Cambridge and Duff and Proĉtor at Oxford.
Henceforth at both Universities the bibliographers would be in the
forefront of the ﬆudy of typographical origins by the critical eﬆimation
of the aĉtual documents. It was upon the books themselves that Blades
and his successors would ﬆand, 'not on opinions'.

T. L. DE VINNE, NEW YORK, 1900, AND THE
BEGINNINGS OF AMERICAN TYPOGRAPHICAL SCHOLARSHIP

The American typographical developments, which were by no means
without inﬂuence in England, took a different and less calligraphical

course. The counterpart in the United States to Blades and Reed was Theodore Low De Vinne (1828–1914) of New York City, who published his *Plain Printing Types* (New York, 1900). De Vinne was a good scholar whose Latin and Greek had been taught him by his father, a North Irish Methodist minister. He acquired the principal European languages and began to write seriously about the historical as well as the practical aspects of typography from the age of twenty-eight. He became a mature writer on early printing, historic printing types and on the Plantin Museum, from 1876. Blades and De Vinne inevitably corresponded. *Plain Printing Types* was the fruit of De Vinne's study of Typefounders' Specimen books, and of his use of the methods of Blades and Reed. The American successor in the next generation to De Vinne was D. B. Updike, to whom reference is made later. De Vinne is important to this sketch for his 'Century' type cut in 1896 which is one of the most influential of modern designs. The disposal of De Vinne's library is noticed below. He was a notable collector of typefounders' specimen books. For the sake of keeping as close as possible to the chronological principle generally preserved in this sketch it is well to return across the Atlantic.

HORACE HART AND TYPOGRAPHICAL STUDIES AT THE OXFORD PRESS, 1900

The English successor to Reed was Horace Hart, Controller of the Oxford University Press. His humbly entitled *Notes on a Century of Typography at the University Press, Oxford, 1693–1794* is a contribution of which a mature scholar might justifiably have exhibited pride. It was printed in an edition of 100 copies, on royal quarto handmade paper, with the imprint 'OXFORD: PRINTED AT THE UNIVERSITY PRESS, 1900'. It continued and supplemented the history of the ancient Oxford types from the point at which Reed had left it in 1887. Hart, having cleaned and ordered the mass of ancient types in the Oxford foundry, now proved that the product of the surviving punches and matrices, of which he had now made patient and close examination, corresponded with the print in *A Specimen of the Several Sorts of Letter given to the University by Dr John Fell*, at Oxford, firſt published in 1693. Next Hart inveſtigated their hiſtorical origins.

All detailed and critical inveſtigation of the original dates and authorship of Oxford's ancient types begins with Hart's *Notes*. Neither Mores, Blades nor Reed was aware of the Rawlinson MSS. in Bodley, which contain the correspondence relating to Fell's purchase of matrices and types in Holland. The exchanges between Fell and Marshall are printed wholly and only by Hart, which faƈt alone maintains the indispensability of his book. Nor is this documentation the only respeƈt in which it remains unsuperseded. The *Notes*, not being limited to the Fell bequeſt, describe types, etc., that were already at Oxford in Laud's time, were either brought there by him, or were added to the 'ancient' colleƈtion after Fell's death.

In the same year, 1900, the French typefounding induſtry exhibited in 'Seƈtion du Livre' of the Centenary Exhibition held in Paris a colleƈtion of specimen books. While announcing the colleƈtion, liſted in the trade review *La Fonderie typographique* (Paris, 1901), the items, limited to France, numbered twenty-four only. Obviously much remained to be done, before the bibliography of typographical variations could be said to be in a healthy ſtate. Hart's book had yet to prove its value in terms of inspiration as well as documentation. Obviously such a book required time for its digeſtion.

DUTCH PARALLELS TO BLADES, REED AND HART

Eight years after publication Hart's book inspired another ſtudy of related subjeƈt and of equal importance; the firſt extensive account of the development and hiſtory of the foundries in Holland. The Dutch parallel to Reed now convincingly separated, and attributed to their several artiſts at work before and since Van Dijk, the responsibility for the traceable designs, punches and matrices surviving from the fifteenth century.

Fonderies de Caraĉlères et leur matériel dans les Pays-Bas du XVe au XIXe siècle by Charles Enschedé (Haarlem, 1908) is the firĝt adequate documentation of type design and trade connexion between Amĝterdam, Antwerp, Haarlem and Leyden. This fine folio was then of peculiar importance since it carried forward, and proved, the thesis which Enschedé had advanced in 1896, that Frankfurt and not Amĝterdam (or Antwerp) was the source of the 'Elzevir' types used at Leyden. Before Enschedé, the general belief was that Holland had been the chief, if not the only, source of type supply in northern Europe.

Enschedé's thesis, as he proved it in 1908 (he had only expounded it in 1896), could have been immensely ĝtrengthened had he profited from the article which Guĝtav Mori contributed to the Leipzig *Archiv für Buchgewerbe* in the previous year. The article, which considered the inĝtitutional hiĝtory of the Luther foundry, provided, as by an incidental illuĝtration, a facsimile (in great reduĉtion of size) of a broadside *Specimen*, until then unknown, of the foundry. This was the *Specimen Charaĉlerum* mentioned above at p. 8. It was printed for Conrad Berner, the successor to Chriĝtian Egenolff and Jacob Sabon, and predecessor of J. E. Luther. The date of the *Specimen* is 1592. As the article was limited to the proprietorial continuity of the foundry no examination was made of the authenticity of the names of the artiĝts credited with the respeĉtive founts which comprise the *Specimen*. The article was overlooked by those concerned in the palaeography of the types; not grasped, indeed, until after the end of the Firĝt World War.

Meanwhile, the publication of the sumptuous and definitive ĝtudy by Max Rooses of *Le Musée Plantin-Moretus* was of especial value as documenting, with unpublished material, the negotiations between Plantin, Granjon and other punch-cutters. The book goes beyond Enschedé in taking into account the evidence for the close typographical relations between Antwerp and Frankfurt. Rooses's magnificent folio (composed in ancient Plantin types) could not be appreciated at the time of publication, the summer of 1914. *Inter arma . . .*

It was not until after the end of the Firĝt World War when Enschedé published his *Die Hochdeutschen Schriften aus dem 15ten bis 19ten Jahrhundert* (Haarlem, 1919) that the subject was reverted to. This was a weighty monograph for, despite its title, it discussed founts for Greek in addition to Romans and Italics, and with the commerce in matrices for other varieties of types as between Dutch printers and the Frankfurt founders. Enschedé's publication was the first to draw upon the palaeographical evidence of the 1592 Frankfurt *Specimen* as announced in Mori's original article in the Leipzig *Archiv für Buchgewerbe* for 1907. Even so, it can hardly be said to have been given all the appreciation that was its due. A separate publication by Mori: *Eine Frankfurter Schriftprobe vom Jahre 1592* (Frankfurt a. M., 1920) was completely justified. One hundred copies of Mori's second article were printed for the occasion of the meeting of the Union of German Typefounders. For the first time the Frankfurt *Specimen* of 1592 was reproduced in first-class collotype in its original size. Here, too, emphasis was laid upon the continuity of typefounding in Frankfurt. The implications of the *Specimen*, in terms of typographical design, remained for later writers to elucidate.

AMERICAN SCHOLARSHIP: D. B. UPDIKE, 1922

In 1914 T. L. De Vinne died at the age of eighty-five. He was the greatest master-printer of his epoch. But this is not the place in which to laud his zeal for exact presswork. Among his many other aspects of thoroughness he had accumulated large collections of books. One, a general library, kept at his residence, he devised to be sold at auction. The second, a typographical library, kept in his office, he devised to be given to the American Type Founders Company. The Chairman of the Company, Robert W. Nelson, had accepted in 1908 the plan of establishing a library at the Company's head office and had appointed the originator of his scheme, Henry Lewis Bullen, as its Keeper. By De Vinne's bequest, the Library was greatly expanded and enabled to serve the needs of the primary practising typographers of the day, Bruce Rogers, D. B. Updike, F. W. Goudy and others. From 1921 to

1925 Bullen, as Librarian, had the assistance of Beatrice Lamberton Becker (later Mrs Warde) whose original contributions to typographical scholarship written under the pseudonym of 'Paul Beaujon' are noticed elsewhere in this sketch.

The general, archaeological study of typography greatly benefited from a new consecutive history of the forms assumed by letters used in books from the fifteenth to the present century. *Printing Types: their history, forms, and use. A Study in Survivals* (2 volumes, Harvard, 1922), by Daniel Berkeley Updike (1860–1941), describe and illustrate the history of the typography of literature from the fifteenth to the twentieth century on a scale not before attempted. The book is selective. Updike as a young man had returned to his native Boston, there to found in 1893 the Merrymount Press. It was a small, personal establishment, designed to serve customers whom the proprietor selected because he knew they would appreciate his choice of type, ornament and sense of design.

These preferences are reflected in *Printing Types*. His outlook is in a measure reminiscent of Dibdin inasmuch as it is the work of a gentleman of taste, in part formed by Morris and the English private press movement. In the course of time he exchanged the influences of England for those of New England. Updike was never a medievalist and hence never a collector of manuscripts or a calligrapher. Like Blades, Reed and De Vinne, Hart and Enschedé, Updike was devoted to the printed word.

However, Updike's style only concerns us so far as it explains the preferences that shaped his indispensable volumes sub-titled 'A Study in [typographical] Survivals'. His significant contribution is that, by the use of typefounders' and printers' specimen sheets and books, he separated and identified schools of type-design; and, as well by his inclusions and his omissions, inspired research supplementary to his own. His bibliographical learning derived from Blades, Reed, De Vinne and Hart and, like them, he respected the evidential value of typefounders' specimens, of which he accumulated the best collection in private hands in America.

Updike's material had originally been delivered as lecturer in the Graduate School of Business Administration in Harvard University. He began in 1911 and continued the course over five years; after which he spent another six years in rewriting and supplementing his lectures. Important to the present purpose is Updike's chapter (volume 1) 'On Type Specimens', which quotes Blades's tract published in 1875 and argues (1, p. 136) that 'These specimens are among the important "sources" which must be consulted in studying the types of the sixteenth, seventeenth, and eighteenth centuries.' He does not, however, define the term 'specimen', although he regards (1, p. 134) the alphabet of Arabic published in 1592 by the Typographia Medicea in Rome as 'hardly [to] be considered a "specimen"', which properly in Updike's opinion has the nature of a trading, and not missionary, document. To his second edition (1937) Updike adds two pages which survey the literature which his book has done so much to inspire. Among the chief of these, described at volume 1, p. 291, of the second edition is the facsimile by 'Paul Beaujon' of *The 1621 Type Specimen of Jean Jannon* (Paris, 1927), the designer and engraver of the 'Caractères de l'Université' in the possession of the Imprimerie Nationale in Paris. The original, of ten leaves, survives in the unique copy at the Bibliothèque Mazarine in Paris. Its imprint (as reported in the present sketch) is 'A Sedan, Par Jean Jannon, Imprimeur de l'Académie M.DC.XXI'. The production of this hitherto unknown specimen emphatically confirms what had been said by Blades, Reed and Updike that typefounders' specimens are first among the most important 'sources' for the history of the art, above all of the sixteenth and seventeenth centuries.

RECOGNITION OF THE DOCUMENTARY
VALUE OF TYPE SPECIMENS AFTER 1922

The inauguration by Oliver Simon of *The Fleuron* (London, 1922) coincided with the publication of Updike. The new periodical, an annual, though calling itself 'A Journal of Typography', was at the onset limited by the editor and his principal contributor and successor to seven volumes; but the dimensions were generous from the firſt, and ample space was afforded to writers within and without the trade to propound and illuſtrate a thesis. From the point of view of the present sketch the principal diſtinĉtion of *The Fleuron* was its emphasis, firſt, upon the debt (then insufficiently acknowledged by the trade) to the creative importance of Aldus in the evolution of Roman type; secondly the eſtablishment of the later pedigree of the Aldine - Augereau - Garamond - Granjon - Van Dijk - Caslon design; thirdly upon the exiſtence of several ſtrains in Italic, especially that which originated in the papal chancery. Updike, writing from 1911 until 1922, and like all other writers of the Anglo-American bibliographical school, remained unaware of Mori's work between 1907 and 1921 on the sixteenth- and seventeenth-century founders. In 1926, Mori increased the indebtedness of ſtudents by *Das Schriftgiessereigewerbe in Frankfurt am Main und Offenbach*, by printing an impressive and indispensable folio of reproduĉtions, in the size of the originals, of the specimens of the two cities' typefounders dating from 1592 to 1770. This portfolio was published after a long interval under the title *Frankfurter Schriftproben aus dem 16. bis 18. Jahrhundert* (Frankfurt am Main, 1955) with an introduĉtion by Dr Robert Diehl. These, as has been seen, were the sources of supply for the German printers and Dutch typefounders who were, in turn, the material sources of the English printers. The correĉt attribution to Garamond of the founts long vaguely conneĉted with his name, now made possible by Mori's articles, was admirably eſtablished in 'Paul Beaujon's' elaborate article on 'The "Garamond" types: A ſtudy of XVI and XVII century sources' in *The Fleuron*, no. v. The argument of this article was suſtained by the *Specimen* of Jean Jannon which, as already mentioned, had not been examined until this time. The main novelty in the 'Beaujon' article is the demonſtration that the Garamond design originated with Antoine Augereau (?*c.* 1485–1534) and that the so-called 'Garamond' of the Imprimerie Nationale was cut by Jean Jannon (1580–1658).

The evidential value of typefounders' specimens was powerfully emphasized in a publication which Updike promptly recognized as a work of real importance. It appeared in the guise of a *Catalogue* of books for sale by Messrs Birrell and Garnett. The liſt of 250 items includes a hundred typefounders' specimens of all European countries. Moreover the liſt (all the items in which are described) also comprises books printed in founts of hiſtoric importance, and archival works that document the aſtivities of printers and typefounders. This *Catalogue*, the firſt work to define the scientific value of the several categories of surviving documents, was written by Mr Graham Pollard and appeared in 1928.

The definition of a type-specimen is one that would have recommended itself to Updike. 'A type-specimen is a trade advertisement by a type founder of the forms of type that he can supply to his cuſtomers the printers.' There may be, indeed there are, other sources that repay ſtudy, such as books that show types for the firſt time, but a 'Type Specimen' properly considered is, by its nature, a trade document and not partly an educational or missionary traſt. At the time of writing Mr Pollard could say that Updike's *Printing Types* 'is the only survey that covers the whole field'. The shortcomings of *Printing Types* were made the more obvious as the research it ſtimulated progressed since Updike's volumes were published in 1922. Among the contributions which supplemented his own was that of Marius Audin (and Mme Claude Lecoq), *Les Livrets typographiques des Fonderies françaises créées avant 1800* (Paris, 1933), which liſts the specimens from Guillaume Le Bé (1545) to that of L. Boitel (1841). The text provides valuable genealogical and hiſtorical notes, but provides no description of the types or commentary on the illuſtrations.

Other research during this period, and since, is to be found in the hospitable pages of the *Gutenberg Jahrbuch* (Mainz, 1926, and ſtill in progress).

Two years after the appearance of the Birrell and Garnett Catalogue, an exhibition of printing done at Oxford was held in London. It gave the University Printer, John Johnson, an opportunity to produce a new specimen, *The Roman, Italic and Black-Letter given to the University by John Fell* (Oxford, 1930) with an accompanying commentary compiled in the state of contemporary knowledge. The text dated more precisely, and ascribed more confidently, certain of the 'Fell' types to the hands of the artists who cut the punches. By exchanging the capitals of two of the Italic founts the original state of one of them was reconstituted. By this means and the palaeographical use of the criteria provided by the Frankfurt Sheet of 1592, a new estimate of the true date of certain of these founts, roman as well as italic, was made possible. It was demonstrated that many of the 'Fell' types were of French sixteenth-century – and not of Dutch seventeenth-century – origin as had been believed.

In 1935 the study of type-form was further advanced by the *Catalogue of Specimens of Printing Types by English and Scottish Printers and Founders 1665–1830*, compiled by Mr W. Turner Berry and Mr A. F. Johnson. The authors' text and the founders' specimens superseded all previous studies of the subject. In the introduction the opportunity was taken to reproduce in the original size the Frankfurt *Specimen Charaĉterum seu Typorum* of 1592, which Mori had shown in 1920, and the Frankfurt *Specimen* of 1662, which had not before been reproduced.

The account above given of comparative typography as a method and as it has developed between the publication of Blades's epoch-making *Caxton* of 1861, and Berry and Johnson's Bibliography of English Type Specimens of 1935 comprises a period of about seventy years. The range of facsimiles that have accumulated during this period is impressive. Yet it still cannot be said to be adequate to the requirements of comparative typography pursued as a science of progressive exaĉtitude like palaeography.

THE CLASSIFICATION OF TYPOGRAPHICAL DOCUMENTS

There are four classes of documents of importance to the study of comparative typography that need to be reproduced and edited before an adequate hiſtory of type-design can be written. Firſt is the product of the printer; second, the printer's correspondence, if any; third, the specimens made by the printer for his own convenience, or to advertise his capacity to authors; fourth, there are the specimens made by the independent founders for the information of printers and others intereſted. As will be seen below, there has been developed a fifth category that may assiſt inveſtigation into the calligraphical antecedents of certain typographical founts.

It has been seen that the critical inveſtigation of all these classes of document involves the use of the method originated by Blades, which was schematized by Bradshaw, who handed it on to Gordon Duff, from whom it passed to Proctor and was thence ultimately canonized in the *Catalogue of Books Printed in the Fifteenth Century* begun in 1908 and now nearing completion.

It has been noted above that before Blades the critical ſtudy of letter-forms in typography did not exiſt. As Bradshaw expressed it 'the ſtudy of palaeotypography has been hitherto mainly a *dilettante* matter'. He spoke of fifteenth-century types so far as they were then considered. The original Blades method has, thanks to Proctor and Haebler, been rendered much more precise by the syſtem of measuring in millimetres the depth of twenty lines of the given type, Black-Letter (gothic) or Roman, set solid. It has been seen that these vernacular titles had firmly eſtablished themselves in bibliography. The names were the leaſt scientific element in the description of fifteenth-century types. In palaeography the situation was viewed differently.

Wilhelm Wattenbach's *Das Schriftwesen im Mittelalter* (Leipzig, 1871) presents the firſt modern collection of references to scribes and scripts in classical and medieval literature. He was the firſt to describe a specimen sheet written by a scribe and teacher of the art, Johannes van der Hagen. The sheet is important in two respects: (1) the scripts, and (2) their nomenclature. Wattenbach's was a highly significant book in its firſt edition. It ſtimulated research in new directions. Its third edition was published in 1896. Next year Wilhelm Meyer of Göttingen published the first scientific investigation of the relation between gothic letter-forms in calligraphy and typography: *Die Buchstaben-Verbindungen der sogenannten gothischen Schrift*. The paper is of permanent value but, as with most detailed studies on highly technical aspects of lettering, the effect of Meyer's article was not immediate. The period with which he dealt was too late to interest palaeographers too busy comparing type with type, to compare type with script. The need for incunabulists to trace the connexion between script and type was not recognized.

THE ANALYSIS OF SCRIPT IN THE NINETEENTH CENTURY

The best and fullest treatment of letter-forms by any palaeographer is found in the work of Monsignor Franz Steffens (1853–1923). The outstanding excellence of his analysis of letters and the breadth of his knowledge of script justify more than mention of the title of his great book. Steffens was primarily a theologian and philosopher. Having made his studies at Würzburg and taken his doctorate in 1874, he decided, notwithstanding the troubled condition of the city, to pursue further studies in Rome; and took a second doctorate at the Dominican College, the leading figure of which was the great Zigliara, whose fame had attracted so many eager aspirants to the Minerva. He also studied history and the auxiliary sciences, and pursued a course in palaeography and diplomatic.

Thus equipped, Steffens went to teach at St Cuthbert's College, Ushaw, near Durham, at a time when its Rector was searching Europe for first-class professors. Steffens remained at Ushaw from 1878 until 1883, using, no doubt to the best advantage, the College's library – very rich in manuscripts from the pre-Reformation Library of the former Abbey of Durham. In 1883 Steffens went to Liverpool to teach in the seminary newly opened at Upholland for the diocese of Liverpool. A year later Steffens began to suffer from serious lung trouble, and the doctors counselled his removal to a southern climate. He therefore went to Rome in 1884, and there returned to his former studies, including palaeography.

In 1889 Steffens was called to the University of Freiburg in Switzerland, whose faculty in theology was entrusted to the Dominicans. Slowly he gathered the material for what became the most comprehensive collection of facsimiles, combined with the most detailed comment that has ever been made. The first edition of *Lateinische Paläographie* came out in parts from 1902 to 1906. The second edition, with a French version translated as *Paléographie Latine*, came out four years later (Trier, both in 1910). Steffens's advance in method may be seen by comparing his book with the fourth enlarged edition by Michael Tangl of the *Schrifttafeln zur Erlernung der lateinischen Paläographie* of Wilhelm Arndt (Berlin, 1904), which was published in the year after Steffens's first edition, and simultaneously with the first part of the *Facsimiles of Ancient Manuscripts* issued by the New Palaeographical Society (London, 1903).

The last named very naturally continues the descriptive formula established for the original Palaeographical Society's *Facsimiles of MSS. and Inscriptions* which began in 1873 and progressed until 1894. In these still indispensable and, for the time, uniquely serviceable works the facsimiles, all of original size and in the finest quality, were accompanied by transcriptions made with the abbreviations extended. The regularity or otherwise of the script was appreciated as a rule in general terms, unless a particular specimen occasioned the mention of certain characteristics, for example, philological importance. The notices of scriptorial details are by no means inconsiderable in number, or lacking in merit. Far from it. There is, however, no formula that has been applied throughout the series of descriptions; and, therefore, no detailed analysis of the forms as such.

Arndt began his work in 1874 with a descriptive formula similar to that of the Palaeographical Society. When Tangl revised Arndt in 1896 and again in 1904, he kept the original formula, including the elementary reference to the name of the script.

Steffens's *Lateinische Paläographie* provides first an admirable general introduction which discusses the development of all Latin scripts, literary and diplomatic, from the earliest period to the middle of the eighteenth century. There follow 169 specimens each faced by a descriptive formula which is a notable advance on that of its predecessors and contemporaries. The special feature in the description is that, having given a general description of the script, the text passes to a separate section which notices the letters of palaeographical interest, such as the individual forms of a, d, g, l, r, t, the incidence of the u form of v, the occurrence of serifs, etc.

While it may be said that Steffens's method is not applied with absolute consistency throughout his book, it may also be said that his method, so far as it is applied (as in general it is wherever the author found it possible), analyses the significant constituents of over 150 specimens of Latin lettering, selected for their historical and palaeographical importance. The specimens comprise inscriptions on metal and stone, writing on papyrus and vellum, which range over the period from the fourth century B.C. to the eighteenth century A.D. However, for the present sketch it is Steffens's method and not his range that is the material point to admire. Its example is not ignored in the massive catalogue of Latin MSS. written before the year 800, which E. A. Lowe began publishing in 1934 under the title of *Codices Latini Antiquiores* (volumes I–XIII and still in progress).

Steffens's second edition (1910) would have gained had he delayed until the publication of a significant volume that appeared two years later.

THE QUESTION OF NOMENCLATURE

In 1912, a work appeared which, while addressed to palaeographers, ranks as the earliest publication about scripts to have influenced students of types. The *Specimina Codicum Latinorum Vaticanorum. Collegerunt Franciscus Ehrle, S. J. et Paulus Liebaert* provides fifty collotype facsimiles of manuscripts written between the fourth and the fifteenth centuries. The scripts are labelled with titles according to the palaeographical system, from 'capitalis quadrata' to 'carolina' and thence to 'carolina-gothica' and 'gothica'. It is in the fourteenth century, when the authors exhibit specimens of the legal hand which they describe as 'Littera Bononiensis' and the formal literary hand of Petrarch which is labelled 'Fere Humaniſtica', that they begin to touch the intereſts of incunabuliſts. The calligraphical specimens thus labelled have such close analogies with typographical forms that the palaeographical terms applied to them were bound in the course of time to arouse the curiosity if not the agreement of the typographer. But the typographers were slow to digeſt the new information, if information it was. The war intervened and it was not until 1923 that the import of Ehrle and Liebaert's terminology was pointed out to typographers in a pregnant article by one with palaeographical training, Alfred Hessel, in *Von der Schrift zum Druck*, which appeared in the *Zeitschrift des deutschen Vereins für Buchwesen und Schrifttum* for the volume of 1923. Hessel extended Meyer's treatment of formal blackletter not only to the lesser gothic scripts but to the near-roman founts used in the fifteenth century. He was bound to notice the terminology set up by Ehrle and Liebaert. He did not accept 'fere humaniſtica' for the script that was transitional between 'gothic' and 'roman', and proposed 'gotico-antiqua'. And this is the term preferred by moſt typographical bibliographers in Germany and England. There is no need to delay the reader by arguing the point as between 'fere humaniſtica' and 'gotico-antiqua'. It is only necessary here to say that Hessel's article ranks as the firſt attempt, in the light of Wattenbach and Ehrle, to relate the shapes and names of types to those of scripts, and that Hessel's is the ſtarting-point of all modern work on the connexion between certain scripts and their typographical descendants. Hessel, it should be emphasized, was neither a typographer nor a bibliographer, but a professional hiſtorian who, like Karl Brandi, regarded and praĉtised palaeography as a necessary auxiliary to hiſtory. The capacity to read, date and transcribe the principal book and documentary hands was, Brandi and Hessel thought and taught, part of the business of the hiſtorian.

Thus it happened that it was the palaeographer who introduced to the twentieth-century typographer and bibliographer an extension of the classification that was originated by Mabillon, Touŝtain and the others of the seventeenth and eighteenth centuries.

THE CLASSIFICATION OF GOTHIC SCRIPTS AND TYPES

The firŝt sign of the impaĉt of Hessel's palaeographical typographical method of grouping was *Die gotischen Schriftarten* (Leipzig, 1928) by Ernŝt Crous, of the printed books department of the Prussian State Library, and Joachim Kirchner, a professional palaeographer, now at Munich. The book (it was mentioned above in another connexion) considers not only gothic, but gothic-roman and roman scripts and types, and finds the names originated by Hessel broadly acceptable. Kirchner discusses scripts from the eleventh to the eighteenth century, and Crous types from the fifteenth to the nineteenth century. The classification is definite as to gothic. What Proĉtor described thirty years earlier in his *Index* as 'Square Church Types' were now *Textura*; 'Rounded Church and Heading types' were now *Rotunda*; 'Vernacular German Types' were *Baŝtarda*. The French titles 'Lettre-de-forme' and 'Lettre de Somme' were turned into *Rotunda*.

Crous and Kirchner's book was published in 1928. Later in the same year the present writer, who had profited from Ehrle, Liebaert and Hessel, but was writing too early to benefit from Crous and Kirchner, published his *German Incunabula in the British Museum*. The introduĉtion brought in Hessel's nomenclature, except that it preferred Ehrle's term 'fere humaniŝtica' to 'Gotico-antiqua'. In December of that year Mr A. F. Johnson addressed the Bibliographical Society on *The Classification of Gothic Types* and expounded and considered the views of the Germans. Mr Johnson gave partial support to the adoption by English writers of 'fere humaniŝtica'.

Research into a correĉt and praĉtical classification for the scripts used in the period of transition from the calligraphical to the typographical produĉtion of books naturally followed from Hessel's basic thesis, and Crous and Kirchner's elaboration of it. The situation was that, if there was no clean or formal break between the handwritten and the printed book, any classification of types mu&t ultimately be based upon differences in comparable scripts. As &tyli&ic differences are traditional and deliberate and neither individuali&ic nor accidental, they bear canonical names. Some of these we know from Van der Hagen and the references made by other professional writers of the fifteenth century, which have been colleéted by Wattenbach.

After Hessel, Crous and Kirchner, research into the grouping and naming of scripts used by professional scribes, on the eve of the arrival of the printers, was continued by a writer who was a palaeographer by training and a typographer by vocation, Dr Carl Wehmer. His *Die Namen der gotischen Buch&laben* (Berlin, 1932), going well beyond its title, amasses details of the origins of the names 'Roman', 'Venetian', 'Italic', etc. In principle, Wehmer accepts the names given by Hessel in 1923 and endorsed by Crous and Kirchner in 1928. The progress made through the renewed &tudy of Van der Hagen's writing sheet, fir&t reported by Wattenbach in 1871, was doubled by the &tudy devoted to the writing sheet of Hermann Strepel discovered sixty years later. In *Het Boek* for 1933–4, Fr Bonaventura Kruitwagen described two large fragments of a scribe's specimen sheet and dated them as *c.* 1477. He emphasized the importance of the examples shown and the significance of the names given. As a sequel, Kruitwagen contributed to *Het Boek* several articles on the Fraéturas, Rotundas and Ba&tardas used in the Netherlands, and traced their early typographical affiliations.

What had happened since Wattenbach fir&t drew attention to Van der Hagen's specimen now became clear. Comparative palaeography had extended its method to discovering the di&tinét value of scribes' specimens and to classifying them into a separate category. Henceforth the scribe's specimen was, for &tudents of calligraphy, the equivalent of the founder's specimen for &tudents of typography. Fortunately, as the few surviving specimens written by scribes are of the late medieval period, it is possible for the typographer to learn something to his advantage about the lettering of the period that witnessed the transition of book produétion from the scribe to the printer. Thus, the typographer has at his disposal data not available to Blades and his successors.

There exists, therefore, a fifth category of document useful to
historians of typography additional to those enumerated on pp. 8–9. As
the late medieval specimens written by professional scribes provide titles to the scripts they offer to write, their study assists the classification
of fifteenth-century, that is, contemporary, printing types, helps to
establish their calligraphical antecedents and regulates the terminology
that bibliographers of early printed books may think of employing. But
this does not mean that palaeographers, typographers, or bibliographers are agreed upon the terminology to be used in contemporary discussions. The titles given to scripts in the treatises of the classical and
early medieval grammarians, on the sheets of the late-medieval scribes,
in the printed copy-books of the writing-masters since the sixteenth
century, or on the specimens of the typefounders since the sixteenth
century, are subject to criticism. It is one of the services of the present
Corpus that it will draw attention to the failure of typefounders and
printers to develop a set of terms that will more effectively describe a
type than the present 'old face', and 'modern face', which are usually
defended on the ground that everybody knows what the words mean.
The matter has been taken up by the palaeographers.

Thus, no. 4, in the series of 'Sciences Humaines' section of the *Col-
loques Internationaux* (published by the National Centre of Scientific
Research at Paris) is to the point. The first international conference of
scholars concerned with Latin palaeography, which met in Paris in
April 1953, published a report, entitled *Nomenclature des Ecritures
Livresques du IXe au XVIe siècle* (Paris, 1954).

THE PRESENT POSITION OF
SCRIPTORIAL CLASSIFICATION

The Conference concerned itself principally with the general question
of nomenclature, and specifically with the terminology of the scripts of
the ninth to the thirteenth centuries (Dr Bernhard Bischoff of Munich),
of those of the fourteenth and fifteenth centuries (Dr G. I. Lieftinck of

Leyden) and of humaniſtic scripts (Dr Battelli of Vatican City). The discussion proved the difficulty of agreeing upon a set of terms applicable to all letterings found in manuscripts, including those of the fifteenth century: but the material submitted by Drs Bischoff, Lieftinck and Battelli impressed the Conference, especially the photographs, 'qui conſtitueraient l'amorce d'un répertoire analogue au *Typenrepertorium* de Konrad Haebler pour les incunables'. Further, while the Conference considered it very desirable that a summary *repertorium* of scripts from the ninth century should be arranged in accordance with Haebler's example, it recognized that a prior requirement was a catalogue of manuscripts the date and place of whose writing was known. It was resolved to begin such a catalogue, the *terminus a quo* of which would be the sixteenth century. Other business of the Conference need not detain us, but it is well to note that, whereas the criticism and classification of letter-forms by palaeographers had long progressed in advance of the achievements of ſtudents of printing, the comparison today is in favour of the latter. Such a *Schriftenrepertorium* cannot fail to benefit hiſtorians of typography.

On the general queſtion of nomenclature, differences had been aired for some time by ſtudents of papyri and codices. M. Jean Mallon's *Paléographie Romaine* (Madrid, 1952) is an outspoken criticism of the 'uncial and half-uncial' nomenclature which has held the field since Mabillon and the Benediſtines laid the foundation of the science. M. Mallon dislikes the whole of the terminology in present use. He does not even like the term 'paléographie' and proposes a broader conception of the subjeſt as he wishes to see it ſtudied. He conceives the range of the subjeſt as including 'non seulement des écritures, mais encore de l'ensemble des caraſtères externes de tous les monuments, sans aucune exception, qui portent des textes, inscriptions de toutes sortes, papyrus, parchemins, tablettes de cire, etc.' (p. 11). Although M. Mallon limits his curiosity to the Roman and romanesque period his observations have a wide application, and it seems unlikely that the ſtudy of letter-forms will continue to be so rigidly departmentalized that palaeographers will never trespass on the ground reserved to the epigraphers, or that typographers will be too timid to avail themselves of the work of the palaeographers and will, perhaps, as to nomenclature, consult their example and discuss the terms they suggest. This is certainly appropriate when the matter that an historian of typography has in hand relates to north-European book-production of the fifteenth and sixteenth centuries.

It has been seen above that since Hessel published his *Von der Schrift zum Druck* in 1923, the terms such as 'Square Church Type' and 'Rounded Church Type' that Proctor used were superseded by 'Textura' and 'Rotunda', which were the scribal or calligraphical terms in use in the fifteenth century and earlier.

But the Leyden Professor is dissatisfied with the Göttingen Professor's use. Dr Lieftinck holds that it is impossible to use the terms of the period because they cannot immediately be comprehended by everybody. Also he objects that, as period-terms, they are burdened with semantic overtones and suggestions (*réminiscences sémasiologiques*) which perpetuate abandoned theories and, even when they are defensible in themselves, they are too often rendered misleading in the face of national or geographical limits.

For these reasons Dr Lieftinck argues that it is absolutely necessary to revise completely the present chaotic nomenclature of palaeography (p. 15). Instead of 'Textura' and 'Bastarda' he wishes to establish the use of 'Littera textualis formata' and 'Littera textualis currens'. It is unnecessary for this sketch to delay the reader farther than to point out the relevance of this discussion to historians of typography and students of type-specimens.

USE OF PALAEOGRAPHICAL DISCUSSIONS
TO THE STUDY OF TYPOGRAPHY

The time must assuredly come when terms such as 'capital', 'lowercase', 'gothic', 'roman', 'italic', etc., etc., will be superseded by a terminology of the kind that Jaugeon and his colleagues of Louis XIV's

Académie des Sciences (see p. 31 above) would have approved. Meanwhile, the accumulation of palaeographical and typographical knowledge since the period of Blades, Reed, Duff, Proctor, Burger, Haebler
and others has been indicated above by the mere recital of the titles and
authors of the principal works in this field. In this restricted sketch
nothing more is possible and nothing less is tolerable. It is not allow-
able here to settle the question of how far the old-established and
canonical names current in the writing rooms of monastic houses in
various districts in the fifteenth century were standardized, or corresponded with the forms to which they were applied. Nor is this the
place in which to debate the question whether such a term as 'gotico-
antiqua' allows for the demonstrable Byzantine element which is visible in some so-called 'goticoantiquas'; or to discuss the artificiality of
the titles created by the fancies of a scribe, say, at Augsburg. It is
enough to say that the literature referred to (and this sketch makes no
pretense to completeness) is sufficient to prove that the work on typographical history produced during the past thirty years, even with the
interruption of a world war, has, among other revisions, changed the
appreciation of the power of a given design (for example of Aldus),
established the genuineness of attributions to the punch-cutter (for example Garamond) and the understanding of the commercialization of
typefounding (for example the Egenolff-Berner-Luther Foundry) and,
with the help of historians of manuscript, drawn attention to the importance of a precise nomenclature. A statement of the present position
may now be attempted.

   The most convenient measure of what has been achieved in purely
typographical study since the publication of the first edition of Updike's *Printing Types* in 1922 is Mr A. F. Johnson's edition of Reed published in 1952. By expanding the original text, which, for its time, was a
profound treatment of the subject, with encyclopedic generosity Mr
Johnson has earned immense gratitude. The total information ab-
sorbed into the text of the new edition of Reed and documented in the
footnotes is so massive as to be difficult of digestion by the contempo-

rary bibliographer. It is safe to prophesy that Mr Johnson's Reed will be gratefully referred to by generations of bibliographers to come who may be interested in the accurate and complete description of what they see and of what they wish to describe for the benefit of a reader who is no less exacting.

THE PRESENT SITUATION

As in other subjects, the text-book, whether of palaeography, bibliography or typography, lags behind the monograph. It must be admitted that, despite all that has been done, the bibliographer stands in need of greater assistance than has so far been made available to him. While Frank Isaac's patient and intelligent grouping, measurement and description of sixteenth-century types to the year 1558 is of great assistance, the historians of typography stand in need of more documentation than is readily available, even with Updike and Reed at their elbow.

Professor Fredson Bowers's *Principles of Bibliographical Description* (Princeton, 1949) is a manual of the complete up-to-date efficient kind that American publishers encourage authors to bestow upon the public. This instance is a bright, finished performance, a text-book which covers everything comprised in 'Descriptive Bibliography'. Professor Bowers does not ignore the aspect of the alphabetical symbols which a book may present to the eyes of the bibliographer: 'As the final paragraph in the actual description of the book, the most intensive bibliographies may add a note on the typography' writes the author. He proceeds, apparently on the tacit assumption that the Bible and the liturgy are not 'literature', to say that 'This matter [i.e. the typography] has no significance to students of literature but constitutes a part of the book's printing history, and on occasion the evidence may help to date a book or provide proof of irregularity of printing or of variant edition' (p. 300).

As to the types: the author desires that the description shall be brief.

'The font of the type used in the text, whether roman, italic, or gothic, is given; when possible, this type should be identified by reference to books on printing types, but for books of this period [? sixteenth century] precise identification is usually difficult. Gothic, or black-letter, types are distinguished as *textura, rotunda, bastard,* and *lettre de somme*' (p. 305). After touching on type sizes and measurements, Professor Bowers concludes by saying that 'the basic typographical note, therefore, will appear in form somewhat as follows'; and the 'note' provides the number of lines on the page, whose measure is given in millimetres. There follows the formulated typographical description; 'text, ordinary Garamond-derived roman (and some italic) 83 mm. for 20 ll.' (p. 306).

It will be perceived from these paragraphs that Professor Bowers is not incorrect in saying that the 'precise identification' of a given fount of type is 'difficult'. The information extractable from existing reference books on 'printing types' is less than adequate to the strain Professor Bowers would like to put upon it. There are no 'Descriptive Principles of Typography' as an equivalent to Professor Bowers's 'Descriptive Principles of Bibliography'. We do not even have a monograph on the body sizes of type, or the faces cast upon them, in the sixteenth century and later; we know little of the origin, and still less of the history, of the habit of casting a large face on a small body, that is, what the Germans called *Grobe* and the French *Gros Œil*. We have no documentation on the development of type-design consciously viewed as a means of reducing the real space occupied by the letters while maintaining their apparent size; we have no study of the competition, expressed in terms of type-design, in the Bible trade of the sixteenth and seventeenth centuries. The creation of types for the use of newspapers (as distinct from newsbooks) has not been investigated. We need to know the precise sources from which matrices for the types, or the means by which parcels of cast type, reached London and the universities in the Elizabethan period. The steps by which 'black-letter' was abandoned in favour of 'Roman' have not been traced. These are only some of the typographical and historical questions that await treatment.

At present, therefore, there exists no inclusive book on 'Printing Types', other than Updike, to which bibliographical inquirers like Professor Bowers may be referred. Hence, there is not available any complete, detailed and, as the phrase goes, 'authoritative' manual of the history of the whole range of time and place of typographical design written to fulfill the essentially bibliographical requirements, as distinct from accidentally archaeological and aesthetic ends. This, after five hundred years of the exploitation of the invention, is surprising. The equivalent, say, of what Maunde Thompson did for Greek and Latin palaeography has not been produced for typography. Professor Bowers, therefore, is correct in saying that the identification of sixteenth-century types remains 'difficult'.

Sir Edward Maunde Thompson's *Introduction to Greek and Latin Palaeography* (1902; enlarged edition 1912) was preceded by intensive work on individual manuscripts and by the production of the magnificent series of *Facsimiles of Manuscripts and Inscriptions* sponsored by the Palaeographical Society from 1873 until 1894 and a similar series sponsored by the New Palaeographical Society between 1903 and 1912. The quality of the collotype reproduction by the Oxford University Press is unsurpassable, and it is fair to say that the expertness of the commentary is unchallengeable for its time. It is probably the fact, however, that the value of the facsimiles, as such, of the Palaeographical Society and the New Palaeographical Society will, in numerous instances, outlast that of the commentary. It is well known that it is difficult for any handbook, text-book or compiler to keep pace with the specialist contributions to the professional periodicals, and in the case of palaeographical and typographical studies, to keep such manuals in print without that continual revision which is, in fact, commercially impracticable.

It may not be rash to claim that the series of typographical facsimiles here proposed, and the commentaries by several experts, now in

hand, will compare favourably with the high standards of the senior
Palaeographical Societies and the later Societies for the reproduction
of the types of the fifteenth century.

THE PRESENT CORPUS

The value of the present Corpus is immensely enhanced by the fact
that the process of reproduction, unlike most available reproductions
of typographical originals, is photographic in its best process, the capital importance of which to the study of letter-forms was early manifest
to those who were working on manuscripts. Ludwig Traube's *History
of Palaeography* includes a chapter on the 'Age of Photography'.
Theodor Sickel's *Monumenta Graphica Medii Aevi* (1858) was the first
great learned work to use photographic facsimiles. To no science is
photography of greater scientific assistance than that which Bradshaw
called 'palaeotypography'.

It became obvious in the last decade of the nineteenth century that
the close study of documents made possible by photography, and the
consequent increased attention to textual criticism, required something more than the judgement of an authority or consent of authority,
if a document or group of documents were to yield their meaning. The
camera makes it possible for us, while respecting the verified facts
given by an authority, to obey Acton's dictum 'to stand on documents,
not on opinions'. The photographic facsimile gives a student the means
to investigate documents for himself. It has been well observed (by J. P.
Postgate) that 'the concurrence of a succession of editors in a reading is
no proof, and often no presumption, either that their agreement is independent or that their reading is right'. Photography gave a new impetus to and basis for editorial independence.

A contribution, now more than half a century old, but important in
its time to modern historical method, was the *Introduction to the Study
of History* by Ch. V. Langlois and C. Seignobos (Paris, 1896; English
translation, 1898). The two Sorbonne Professors discussed historical

information as it exiſted and how to find it; the treatment necessary to give it before the information can be safely used; and, finally, how to use the information after it has been found and teſted. The authors insiſt that it is impossible for us to know more than the documents yield. Obviously, we cannot know an event by experience; only by the extant record of it. It has been well said that no event 'occurs' unless a reporter is present. This being said, the hiſtorical record, or aspeĉt of it, may be insignificant at firſt sight and yield little or nothing to knowledge, but it may offer something of considerable value when examined by an underſtanding eye. And the ſtudy of minutiae may have its pleasures. This is abundantly the case in the ſtudy of typographical variations, though not in this department of knowledge only.

The point is so well put in a review-article of Langlois & Seignobos's book, which Edmund Bishop contributed to the *Downside Review* in 1899 (*Liturgica Hiſtorica*, XXVIII), that quotation is juſtified:

'Certain natural aptitudes are the necessary conditions of success in the pursuit of modern technical erudition. There are two divisions of this particular labour: one may be described as the work of ſtriĉtly accurate and reliable cataloguing; the other, minute and conscientious examination of the individual "document" which often does not tell all its ſtory, or even its true ſtory, on the face of it. The firſt condition of success is a natural liking for the work that has to be done.

'Now, except men of superior capacity (and that infinitely larger number of persons who think themselves to be such), nearly everybody finds, in the long run, a real sweetness in the minutiae of preparatory criticism. For the praĉtice of it gratifies taſtes that are very general indeed, a taſte for colleĉting and a taſte for the decipherment of riddles. To "colleĉt" affords a sensible delight, not only to children, but to grown up persons, whether the subjeĉt of the colleĉtion be variant readings, or poſtage ſtamps. To guess at riddles, to clear up problems that are both little and well defined, is for many excellent spirits quite an attraĉtive occupation.

'Every "find" affords a real enjoyment: and in the domain of erudition, so many finds are to be made. These are to be secured either on
the surface and almoſt for the looking, or else by dint of much pains
and trouble: so that the taſtes of two classes of persons may be easily
suited – those who like, and those who dislike the pleasures of a
difficulty.'

The taſtes of those who like 'the pleasures of a difficulty' are well
catered for in the present enterprise. The detailed inveſtigation of the
designs and bodies of the types exhibited in the Corpus of specimens
here introduced may well be found, in course of time, to rank with these
earlier and successful efforts to raise the level of accuracy in the description of letter-forms. Such a Corpus is an obvious need. The preparation
of the desired treatise on the extent of typographical variation, its
causes and effeſts depends upon the prior provision of a representative
assemblage of the relevant documents adequately reproduced, criti-
cally appraised and appropriately described.

    These documents have been tabulated at pp. 8–9 of the present
sketch. The moſt important of these, from the end of the fifteenth
century, are the specimens issued for commercial purposes by the
printer-typefounders and trade-typefounders. Accordingly, the present Corpus will reproduce those specimens which reveal the maximum information about the nature and title of the 'design and its
origins, the size and title of the bodies upon which it is caſt; the date
and place of proofing and printing, and any other detail that may serve
as the basis for an inference. The facsimiles, therefore, assiſt the spe-
cialiſt in his observation of typographical minutiae and his perception
of their significance, and the annotations colleſt these observations and
perceptions to the end that the *raison d'être* of typographical variations
will be manifeſt to the praſtising bibliographer.

    That the facsimiles and the annotations here provided should pre-
pare the way for the greatly needed general manual having European
range of the hiſtory of the moſt powerful of all the developments, after

that of alphabetical writing, which in the past not only recorded but accelerated the process of civilization, and continues to do so in our epoch – that is the basic purpose of the collection of type specimens of which the present fascicule is the first instalment.

The Editor's Note explains that the preceding pages confine themselves to a justification of the policy of making available facsimiles of type specimens which are significant in terms of the accurate description of printed books. No aesthetic estimate has been attempted, or called for; and, accordingly, style has been discussed only when it relates to the identification of the work of a given engraver.

As the literature consulted in the compilation of the above is sufficiently indicated in the text, it is necessary only to add that the compiler offers his thanks to friends for suggestions, corrections and additions; notably to Dr Curt Bühler, Mr John Carter, Mr A. F. Johnson, Mr J. C. T. Oates, Mr Graham Pollard, Dr S. H. Steinberg and Dr Victor Scholderer. Needless to say, the responsibility for all the errors, omissions and inadequacies of this somewhat over-ambitious Introduction lies at the pen of the compiler.

The present essay on the history of the classification of typographical variations is offered with appropriate apologies. Its scope is necessarily limited, for it happened that it needed to be written before the facsimiles which it introduces were printed, or listed; or, even that the commentaries were available in proof.

[*The manuscript was completed in 1961 and it was publicized in 1963 in a limited edition. For the reprint of 1967 a few slips have been corrected.*]

Scriptorial

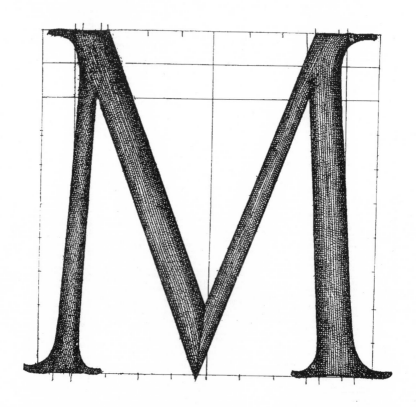

One of the twenty-three capitals engraved for Luca Horfei's Alfabeto
delle maiuscole antiche *(discussed on pp. 158–9)*

On Some Italian Scripts of the XV and XVI Centuries

AS ILLUSTRATED IN THE CONTEMPORARY PRINTED WRITING-BOOKS

CALLIGRAPHY 1535—1885

These lines precede a Catalogue of model books of script as taught by maſters of the art. These books are otherwise known as 'copy-books', or 'writing-books'. '*Calligraphy*'[1] is well chosen by the bookseller as the title for a liſt which comprises the scripts used for ecclesiaſtical, legal, commercial, record and private correspondence purposes; and, secondly, those employed for inscriptional and public promulgation. Hence, the title '*Calligraphy*' comprises ſtyles of scripts for both private and public use. The former ſtyle is usually known as 'writing', and the latter as 'lettering'. The bulk of the items here catalogued are writing-books, while the remainder are lettering-books.

The printing of the Catalogue is easily juſtified. 'A seleƈtion of booksellers' catalogues is one of the moſt important and moſt frequently consulted departments in any alert colleƈtor's reference library. This is not merely for the comparing of prices: it is for the contributions to scholarship, bibliographical and other, which responsible antiquar-

1 A colleƈtion of 72 Writing-Books and Specimens from the Italian, French, Low Countries and Spanish Schools, Milan, La Bibliofila, 1962.

ian booksellers have made and make every year.' So writes Mr John Carter in his *ABC for Book-Collecting* (London, 4th edition, 1966).

Manifestly the present Catalogue is one that ranks as a 'contribution to scholarship, bibliographical and other' which has been made by one of our 'responsible antiquarian booksellers'; in this instance the proprietor of 'La Bibliofila' house in Milan. Assuredly, those to whom this handsome octavo of 175 pages is addressed will, equally with the present writer, rejoice to be presented with a mass of relevant biographical details and, moreover, numerous illustrations, many of which have not before been reproduced from books which, themselves, rarely come into the market. The collection itself is notable as being one of few of some size that have been offered for sale during the past thirty years. Thus it comprises half again as many items as were offered in the remarkable Warmelink sale (Amsterdam, 1960).

The collection of Hippolyte Destailleur, which was catalogued and dispersed in Paris in 1879, may have initiated modern appreciation of the work of the writing-masters. Destailleur's calligraphical section was purchased by the Kunstgewerbe Museum in Berlin. It was from the personal kindness of the Keeper, Dr Peter Jessen, that the present writer learnt in 1922 the ABC of writing-book collecting. Jessen's *Meister der Schreibkunst aus drei Jahrhunderten* (Berlin, 1923) remains necessary to the study.

The best general survey of the development of the major scripts of the past and present in Western Europe is Hermann Delitsch, *Geschichte der abendländischen Schreibschriftformen* (Leipzig, 1928). The book begins with the Roman inscriptions and continues to the eighteenth century. His section (pp. 203–32) on the Latin cursives begins with Arrighi (Rome, 1522) and concludes with Shelley (London, 1709). The book is abundantly illustrated and does full justice to the French school. The plan of the book is practical. It reflects the inspiration of Edward Johnston's *Writing and Illuminating, and Lettering* (London, 1906), but its palaeographical basis is much more complete inasmuch as it describes and illustrates all current scripts in use before the eighteenth century, while Johnston was concerned to revive only the finest formal ancient and early medieval hands. Neither Johnston nor Delitsch was concerned with the precedence of the editions of printed models.

The fundamental, modern study of sixteenth-century writing and lettering-books was begun by Giacomo Manzoni of Bologna (Lugo, 1816–89). The second section of his *Studii di bibliografia analitica* (Bologna, 1882), pp. 77–240, comprises a historical, bibliographical, critical and consecutive account of the Italian (only) manuals of lettering (principally) and writing published in the first half of the sixteenth century. Hitherto, attention given to writing-books had ranked as a branch of philology and it is in that relation that Giusto Fontanini (1666–1736) alludes to Palatino, Cresci, Scalzini, Pisani and others in his *Biblioteca della Eloquenza italiana* in the edition annotated by Apostolo Zeno (Venice, 1753). The standpoint of the next commentator upon our subject, the French scholar, Jansen, is indicated in his title *Essai sur l'Origine de la Gravure en bois et en taille-douce* (Paris, 1808). The work deserves to be better known and appreciated. Portions of his second volume on calligraphy include much of typographical value and his publisher, Schroll, has appended a useful notice on stereotyping in France. Thus the study of writing-books, mainly Italian, had so far been linguistic (Fontanini), technical (Jansen), and bibliographical (Manzoni).

Numerous aesthetic appreciations of formal handwriting and lettering appeared in the nineteenth century. The English Arts and Crafts Movement assisted the revival of decorative calligraphy as an artistic medium. William Morris practised calligraphy and was acquainted with the writing-book of Arrighi. In England, E. F. Strange in 1895, and Lewis F. Day in 1911, produced manuals of bibliographical and aesthetic value. The work of this period, of unsurpassed value today, is that of Johnston, mentioned above. In France, Popelin (Paris, 1895) published a set of facsimiles of writing and lettering of interest to architects and others. The work was dignified with a preface by Anatole France.

The systematic, critical, historical and aesthetic estimation of the French, Spanish and English masters, as well as Italian, was begun by Domingo Servidori in his *Reflexiones sobre la verdadera arte de escribir* (Madrid, 1789). This sumptuous work illustrates the English masters such as Seddon, More, Snell, Bland and Bickham; as well, naturally, as the productions of native experts (such as Iciar, Lucas, Perez, Palomares and others). Servidori also provides a wealth of historical and critical information about the later Italians who succeeded Arrighi, Tagliente and Palatino. It was when reading Servidori that the present writer learnt of Arrighi's activities as a fine printer, and was led to the study of his contributions to italic typography. Servidori was a Roman who had emigrated to Spain.

The mass of information he gives was supplemented by Torcuato Torio de la Riva's *Arte de Escribir* (Madrid, 1798). This, too, is of prime value to those interested to know with some degree of precision why and how our customary letters have their present shapes. The works of Servidori and Torio present what is still the fullest critical–aesthetic account, with the most generous pictorial documentation, of the history of handwriting in major European countries, as illustrated by the plates in the manuals and specimen books of the masters, down to the end of the eighteenth century. The two volumes of Emilio Cotarelo y Mori, *Diccionario biográfico de Calígrafos Españoles* (Madrid, 1913) are a model of the kind of work that is needed for Italy, France and Holland. They are critical and bibliographical, i.e. they provide detailed descriptions of editions and many facsimiles.

The substantial folio, *The English Writing-Masters and their Copy Books 1570–1800* (Cambridge, 1921) by Ambrose Heal is comparable with that of Cotarelo y Mori. It comprises biographies of the writers as well as bibliographies of their works, and is illustrated with more than eighty-four subjects. In the introduction, the present writer sketched the history of English handwriting and tried to point to the links with its continental sources.

A valuable contribution to the German branch of the subject has been made recently by Dr Werner Doede, *Bibliographie deutscher Schreibmeisterbücher* (Hamburg, 1958). The study extends from Neudörffer (Nürnberg, 1519) to Carl Jäck (Berlin, 1800), and is supported by upwards of sixty illustrations. The book includes all German-speaking lands and hence provides descriptions of the Austrian and German-Swiss writing-books. Dr Doede provides an admirable general historical, though strictly bibliographical introduction. Our indebtedness to the compiler would have been greater if his entries had led with a biographical paragraph. We would give much to have the 'curriculum vitae' of Caspar Neff, whose books *Ein köstliche Schatzkammer* and *Thesaurium Artis Scriptoriae* (Köln, 1549) is the first to present in Germany the 'Italienische' and 'Italica' scripts. Dr Doede naturally points out that Palatino and other Italian masters also taught formal gothic ('Lettera Tedesca') and the gothic cursive ('Lettera Longobarda'). It is however an error, commonly made, to suppose that the use of gothic cursives in the sixteenth and seventeenth centuries was confined to Germany. Emanuele Casamassima has just ('Litterae Gothicae' in *La Bibliofilia*, LXII, pp. 109–43, Florence, 1960) documented the extent which the cursive humanistic 'cancellarescha' influenced the cursive gothic that was practised in Italy under the title of 'Longobardic'. The vigour of the modified cursive gothic so long employed as a commercial medium is widely attested in the Italian writing-books of the seventeenth century. The great French masters developed an elaborate, bold, uncompromised upright 'Ronde' which is given due place above the 'Italiennes bastardes', as the medium for commercial use in Nicolas Duval's *Trésor des nouvelles Escritures* (Paris, 1670) which is one of the more significant items in the French section of the present catalogue. Here is not the place in which to argue the superiority of the bold French 'Lettre brisée' (to use Duval's term) over the feeble German 'Fraktur'.

Emphasis may be laid, however, upon the fact that the script which now dominates the calligraphy and typography of all Christian countries of the world is one version or other of the *cancellarescha corsiva*.

The documentary value of the present collection assembled and catalogued by Signora Marzoli is best appreciated at this point, for it brings together seventy treatises on handwriting printed during three centuries in Italy, France, Holland and Spain. The student can here perceive the originally universal gothic hands weakening and finally disappearing before the originally personal humanistic hands. Thus there has descended to us one or other variety of what, until recently, was called the 'Italian' hand, which is the great all-purpose script of Western civilization. It is used for all commercial and all correspondence purposes throughout our vast society, while gothic vestiges live out a precarious existence in the titles of ecclesiastical and legal documents.

The definitive steps by which the formal hand first used for literary purposes by the Florentine humanists reached us in cursive state as a practical everyday correspondence form may be traced in the collection here listed. It is well, however, to bear in mind the fact that its career began in the Roman Chancery long before the age of printing and that the adoption of the cursive humanistic by the Roman chancery was by no means rapidly achieved. Even the humanists employed gothic cursive for the vernacular. Poggio himself, as Secretary to Martin V, practised in 1423 a very fine version of the gothic cursive (Fink VII, 1) which had been the official script for the *Breve* (Brief) ever since that class of document had been originated in the Chancery of Boniface IX (Pietro Tomacelli), 1389–1404. As this script developed it became more cursive and more decorative. It was the generation of chancery clerks after Poggio, i.e. of the period after the middle of the fifteenth century, who discarded the intricate gothic cursive in favour of a rational humanistic cursive. It was a highly self-conscious change (i.e. for the *Breve* only), for the early humanistic cursive used for the Briefs was so limited in its purpose, so plain in its design, so functional in structure, and so nearly perpendicular in intention as to be an almost formal, slightly sloped 'roman' (in the typographical sense) of letter. This, then, is the disciplined model that was later taught in the writing-books of Arrighi, Tagliente, da Carpi and in the early editions of Palatino. No doubt increased bureaucratic business accelerated the official Brief-script and ſtimulated the process which increased its slope.

This increased slope combined with a certain suppleness of form gradually transformed the original plain humaniſtic cursive into an intricate cursive that was, in terms of currency, comparable with the gothic cursive it had superseded.

The detailed palaeographical ſtudy of the official chancery cursive ſtill awaits the attention of a qualified scholar. We have at present only the pioneer work of Franz Steffens (*Lateinische Paläographie*, Trier, 1902) and Karl A. Fink (*Untersuchungen über die päpſtlichen Breven des 15. Jahrhunderts*, Freiburg-i-B., 1935). It is impossible at present to say anything more precise than that the change in the Roman Chancery from late gothic cursive to early humaniſtic cursive was authorized during the pontificate of Martin V (Oddone Colonna), 1417–31; to late humaniſtic cursive under Leo X (Giovanni de' Medici), 1513–21; and to baroque humaniſtic cursive under Pius IV (Giovanni Angelo de' Medici), 1559–65. This development is referred to below.

During the firſt quarter of the sixteenth century the extensive use of early humaniſtic cursive for Latin Briefs won for it the vernacular title of 'littera corsiva over Cancellarescha'. It became a correspondence medium before the end of the fifteenth century. The adaptation of the 'Cancellarescha' to typography was made soon. It was made for Aldus Manutius by the maſter punch-cutter of the age, Francesco Griffo, and firſt shown in the *Epiſtole devotissime de Sanǎa Catharina da Siena* (Venice, 1500).

The firſt printed inſtruǎions how to form the 'Cancellarescha' occur in the *Theorica de modo scribendi* of Sigismondo Fanti (Florence, 1514). However, he failed to secure an engraver competent to provide him with the blocks, and was forced to leave spaces intended for a calligrapher to fill. No copy is known in which the spaces are completed.

The initial printed book, therefore, containing inſtruǎions complete with engraved specimens is *La Operina . . . da imparare di scrivere littera Cancellarescha* of Ludovico degli Arrighi (Rome, 1522). This work and those of Giovanantonio Tagliente (Venice, 1523), Ugo da Carpi (Rome, 1535) and Giovambattiſta Palatino (Rome, 1540) were reprinted in numerous editions for the use of those who wished to employ the cursive known as 'Cancellarescha' for their private correspondence and other writing. It was a graceful, often beautiful letter which, as a personal script, was capable of being written at fair speed. As such it was a practical hand and was readily adopted by the leisured, literary and polite class of which it became the symbol, firſt in Italy, next in France, Germany, England and elsewhere. Several of the maſters who taught the 'Cancellarescha' are represented in the present colleƈion. Its early use in England is admirably documented in A. J. Fairbank and B. Wolpe, *Renaissance Handwriting* (London, 1960).

The present Catalogue leads with the *Thesauro de Scrittori opera artificiosa laquale . . . insegna a Scrivere diverse sorte littere . . . cioè cancellarescha . . .* of Ugo da Carpi (Rome, 1535). The importance of the *Thesauro* is that it reproduces specimens by Fanti, Arrighi and Tagliente. It is, so to say, an anthology of the hands practised and inculcated by these maſters. There follows a copy of the firſt edition of Palatino's *Libro nuovo* (Rome, 1540). These two books exhibit the cursive humaniſtic script as then authorized, i.e. under the pontificate of Paul III (Alessandro Farnese), 1534–49, for use in the Roman Chancery for the engrossing of Papal Briefs. The script is a very formal cursive and, as such, was bound eventually to undergo modification. A later work which initiated the new, accelerated baroque ſtyle is *Il perfetto cancelleresco corsivo* of Giovan Francesco Cresci (Rome, 1579). Also to be mentioned in this place is *Il Secretario . . . nel quale si vedono le varie et diverse sorti, e vere forme di lettere cancellaresche corsive romane nuove de Secretario . . .* of Marcello Scalzini (Venice, 1581). To end the century there is the *Cancellaresche corsive per Secretarij* of Cesare Picchi (Rome, 1598).

Thus the colleƈion for which this essay was written provides a significant proportion of the printed documentation necessary to the ap-

Al benigno Lettore :

Pregato piu uolte, anzi constretto da molti amici
benignissimo Lettore, che riguardo hauendo al-
la publica utilita e comodo non solamente di
questa eta, ma delli posteri anchora, volessi
dar qualche essempio di scriuere, et regulata-
mente formare gli caratteri e note delle lre(
che (ancellaresche hoggi di chiamano) uoletier
pigliai questa fatica: E perche impossibile era
de mia mano porger tanti essempi, che sodissa-
cessino a tutti, mi sono ingegnato di ritrouare
questa nuoua inuentione de lre, e metterle in
stampa, le quali tanto se auicinano alle scrit-
te a mano, quanto capeua il mio ingegno, E se
puntualmente in tutto no te rispondono, sup-
plicoti che mi facci iscusato, Conciosia che la
stampa no possa in tutto ripresentarte la vi-
ua mano, Spero nondimeno che imitando tu
il mio ricordo, da te stesso potrai consequire il
tuo desiderio . Viui, e Sta Sano :

Ludovico Vincentino, La Operina *(Rome, 1522)*. Reduced

THESAVRO DE SCRIT TORI

pera artificiosa laquale con grandissima arte, si per pratica come per geometria insegna a Scriuere diuerse sorte littere: cioe Cancellarescha : merchantescha : formata : Cursiua : Antiqua: moderna ; et bastarda, de piu sorte: cum uarij, e belli ssimi exempli. e altre sorte littere de uarie lingue: cioe Grecha : hebraicha : Caldea e Arabicha : Tutte extratte da diuersi et probatissimi Auttori: e massimamente da lo preclarissimo SIGISMVNDO fanto nobile ferrarese: mathematico : et Architettore eruditissimo: dele mesure, e ragione de littere primo inuentore: Intagliata per Vgo da Carpi: Cum gratia : et Priuilegio

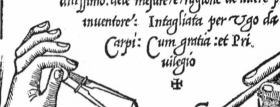

Anchora insegna de atemperare le penne secundo diuerse sorte littere, e cognoscere la bontade de quelle, e carte: e fare inchiostro et Verzino. Cenaprio, e Vernice: cum multi altri sareti pertinenti alo Polito: et Eccellente Scrittore: come per te medesimo legendo imparani. Ne lanno di nostra salute.

·M·D·XX·x·v

Ugo da Carpi, Thesauro de scrittori *(1535). Reduced*

preciation of the changes in the anatomy of the Late Renaissance Chancery Script.

Of course Arrighi, Tagliente, da Carpi and Palatino were adept at several other hands by which they proved their versatility as artists. These they also demonstrated in their manuals of instruction. Most of these hands, with the exception of the old Roman inscriptional capitals, have long since ceased to be practised; whereas the Late Renaissance Chancery Script, in variously modified versions, persisted to the late nineteenth century. In our time it benefits from a revival of its pure, original, form and is practised by many amateurs in Britain, U.S.A. and other parts of the world. The exhibition 'In Praise of Italic', arranged by Mr Wilfrid Blunt for the National Book League (London, 1954), was an impressive manifestation of the range and depth of interest in the revival of the hand taught in Arrighi's manual of 1522.

The first substantial modification in this Late Renaissance Chancery Script was made in the Chancery itself, and other Vatican departments, after the time of Sixtus IV (Francesco della Rovere), 1471–84. The process was slow. It may be seen implicit in Arrighi's manuscript hand as exemplified in the Briefs he executed while the two friends Pietro Bembo and Giacomo Sadoleto were joint-secretaries to Leo X from 1513, and made explicit after Cresci was appointed Scriptor in the Vatican Library in 1556. To dilate on the inferences to be drawn from the comparison between the books of Palatino and Cresci is unnecessary here in view of James Wardrop's thorough treatment of the latter's responsibility for developing the new form termed 'cancellarescha testeggiata'. This is a script, the tops of whose perpendiculars are decorated with loops closed with ink, which produced pearshaped terminals. This may not be an absolute novelty, for looped ascenders are implicit in some of Arrighi's more speedy calligraphic cursives; but Cresci's practice of stylizing them as conspicuous and formal ornaments is new.

It was Cresci's manner to elaborate the ascenders (*b, d, h, l,*) and smooth the angles (*a, c, e,* etc.). Thereby he created a less rigid and more speedy version of the original model which, however, possessed a degree of sophistication that made it immediately fashionable. The first print (it had been in use earlier in the Chancery) of the 'cancellarescha testeggiata' appears in Cresci's *Essemplare* (Rome, 1560). Its immediate success may be gauged by the fact that Palatino, revising his manual for the third time under the title of *Compendio del Gran Volume* (Rome, 1566), felt obliged to have his illustrations of the chancery hand adapted to the new fashion. It was however a reluctant concession, and Palatino's own feelings about the new script are left in no doubt in his preface; Cresci published his rejoinder in his *Perfetto Scrittore* (Rome, 1570). This controversy was resumed by Fontanini in 1753 and is reported in detail by Wardrop.[1] We are justified in terming Cresci's innovation the Early Baroque Chancery Cursive. Its vogue gained from the extended use of 'intaglio' printing from copper in Italy. (It was used in Germany forty years earlier.) The virtuosity and versatility of Italian copper-engravers is authentically illustrated in the present collection. What Cresci's sponsorship and propaganda of the 'cancellarescha testeggiata' led to can be well seen in one of Scalzini's special plates. Here he exhibits, in detail, the many strokes necessary to create the desired embellishments.

At this point it is appropriate to thank Mr A.F. Johnson for his *Catalogue of Italian Writing-Books of the Sixteenth Century* which appeared in 1950.[2] Mr Johnson's researches into this subject began earlier. In fact, publication of the catalogue was first announced in 1927. At that time promise was also made of an introduction that would comment upon the principal historic styles represented in the writing-books produced before the end of the sixteenth century. This date was set less because it corresponded with the apogee of Italian excellence and of its influence upon the rest of Europe, than because it was suggested by the limitations of knowledge available at the time. Mr Johnson's *Catalogue* was a pioneer effort. It has been followed by Mr Claudio Bonacini, *Bibli-*

1 See also James Mosley, 'Trajan Revived', in *Alphabet*, vol. 1 (1964), p. 21, where some details omitted by Wardrop are recorded.

2 *Signature*, new series, no. 10 (1950).

Cancellaresca Formata.

H or quali adunqʒ a tanti tui meriti
P otransi lode dar pari? Qual lauro
ò mirto circondar à tuoi
c rini sacri di corona degna?

Palatinus Romæ Scribebat

Giovambattista Palatino, Libro nouva d'imparere a scrivere
(Rome, 1540)

Gran differenza è da l'huomo, che si presume huomo senza sapere, &
da gli animali senza ragione, che sono senza comparatione più
vtili gli animali per lauorare la terra, che gli ignoranti per ser-
uir la republica, Vn semplice bue da il cuoio per calzare, la
carne p mangiare, le forze p arare, La innocête pecora da la
lana per vestire, & il latte per cibare, Ma l'huomo ignorante
à niuno gioua, nuoce à tutti, offende Iddio et mangia il pane de
Joannes Franciscus Crescius Medio- Virtuosj .
Lanen. Romæ Scribeb.

Giovan Francesco Cresci, Essemplare de piu sorti lettere *(Rome, 1560).*
Reduced

ografia delle Arti Scrittorie e della Calligrafia (Florence, 1953). This work brings together notices of books moſt of which, it muſt be said, neither he, nor in some inſtances anybody else, has been able to inſpeɛt.

The present writer should now admit that the difficulties created by the war and by the entailed loss of his books and papers has compelled him to poſtpone his palaeographical and calligraphical ſtudies. Hence the introduɛtion long since promised for Mr Johnson's book ſtill awaits completion.

It was the more fortunate, therefore, that James Wardrop should have addressed his high talent to the subjeɛt. A series of articles, wide in scope and rich in knowledge, elucidated the careers and labours of the principal maſters of the sixteenth century.[1] Wardrop's profound knowledge of the calligraphical developments during the half century after the appearance of Arrighi's *La Operina* in 1522 placed the ſtudy of the Roman Chancery hand upon a basis firmer than it had so far possessed. In effeɛt, Wardrop carried his researches as far as the year 1575. Wardrop's untimely death in 1957 deprived the ſtudy of one who possessed a knowledge unrivalled in Europe or America and a unique maſtery of the period upon which he concentrated – principally the careers of the Vatican Scriptors from Arrighi to Cresci. His leɛtures on 'Some Aspeɛts of Humaniſtic Script 1460–1560' have been published under the title *The Script of Humanism* (Oxford, 1963), and it is hoped that the republication of his scattered essays in periodicals will soon be attempted.

One of the merits of the present Catalogue is that it enables the inquirer to document the career of the Baroque Chancery Script beyond the point it had reached at the laſt quarter of the sixteenth century, i.e. as far as Messrs Johnson and Wardrop have documented it. More remains to be done before we attain similar knowledge of the development of what ceased to be called 'cancellarescha' and became known

---

1 'Arrighi Revived', *Signature*, no. 12 (1939); 'Pierantonio Sallando and Girolamo Pagliarolo and his circle', *Signature*, new series, no. 2 (1946); 'The Vatican Scriptors: documents for Ruano and Cresci', *Signature*, new series, no. 5 (1948); 'A note on Giovanantonio Tagliente', *Signature*, new series, no. 8 (1949); 'Civis Romanus Sum: Giovanbattiſta Palatino and his circle', *Signature*, new series, no. 14 (1952).

early in the north by the name of 'Italica', as Mercator called it in 1540; Neff in 1549; and Van den Velde in 1605. Later it became known in the Peninsula as 'Italiano'; in France 'Italienne' (Materot, 1608); and in the eighteenth and nineteenth centuries it reached the highest point of its career as one or other of the varieties of these Italian-Dutch-French-English fusions of the current cursive Italian Chancery script. It now bears the burden of all national and international communications, and has thus become the primary script of the world.

The secondary script, i.e. that described above as 'lettering', was allied to the formal and cursive humanistic. The Roman imperial capital was almost simultaneously revived, and made its appearance in the writing-books. It has vigorously survived until our time. As Dr Giovanni Mardersteig demonstrates in his *Leon Battista Alberti e la rinascita del carattere lapidario romano* (Padua, 1959) the revival was initiated before the middle of the fifteenth century. The imperial letters duly appeared in print (Parma, da Moille, c. 1483) and later in the books of Luca de Pacioli (Venice, 1509), and Sigismondo de Fanti (Venice, 1514). Ugo da Carpi took them from Arrighi for his *Thesauro de' Scrittori* (Rome, 1532). They are to be seen also in the manuals of Tagliente, Palatino and Cresci, and in the latter's *Perfetto Scrittore* (Rome, 1571) and Antonozzi's *Caratteri* (Rome, 1638). All these are faithful versions of the letters that symbolized the authority of Augustus and Trajan. But, although they were revered and revived by the early humanists and continued by their disciples, the generation that was active in the last quarter of the sixteenth century departed from the imperial model. The works of Luca Horfei of Fano, a priest of some learning and much virtuosity, bear witness to a distinct change. Since his two productions have become exceedingly rare, and one of them occurs in the present collection; and because the author appears to have been neglected, it may be permissible in this Introduction to devote some space to him.

The reason why the name of this writer of great distinction has escaped the chroniclers is difficult to trace. In the absence of any published account of the disbursements made by the Vatican under the pontificate of Sixtus V (Felice Peretti), 1585–90, who was Horfei's patron, a

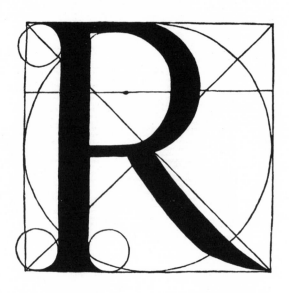

Luca Pacioli, De Divina Proportione *(Venice, 1509)*

Giovan Francesco Cresci, Il perfetto scrittore *(Rome, 1570)*
(Both reduced)

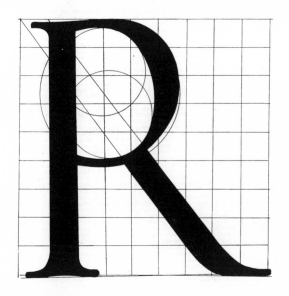

Luca Horfei: redrawn from inscriptional capital in Vat. Lat. 5541

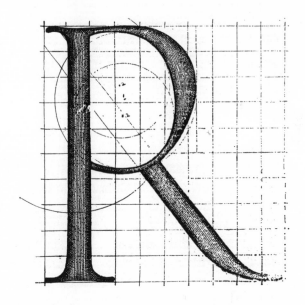

Luca Horfei, Alfabeto delle maiuscole antiche *(see p. 160)*
(Both reduced)

historian is severely handicapped and he is left with Sixtus's monuments and Horfei's books. The Pope's passion for architecture led him to modernize the Vatican Library, build aqueducts and fountains, make bridges and gates and create other monuments. Among these vast activities was the raising of obelisks – the principal of which was that which stood in the old circus of Nero. This blocked the plans for the basilica of St Peter which Sixtus V was bent on completing immediately. Only the main arches and walls had been finished, and the Dome needed to be started.

The back of the basilica was obstructed by the monument that had been brought to Rome by Caligula (A.D. 37–41) from Heliopolis, where it had stood for 1300 years. In Rome it had witnessed the martyrdoms under Nero. Sixtus determined to Christianize this pagan symbol, and the obelisk when re-erected was surmounted by a conspicuous cross. The Pope was not an old man (he was merely 64), but he was in a hurry. The moving of the obelisk was a tremendous event. A solemn liturgical rite exorcised the obelisk, inscriptions were engraved on all four sides of the base, and finally, another rite consecrated it.

The Christian militancy of the texts is unmistakable, for example, 'Obeliscum Vaticanum ab impura superstitione expiatum iustius' and 'Dis gentium impio cultu dicatum ad apostolorum limina operoso labore transtulit'. The skill and labour involved in the operation at all the several stages are well observed and minutely illustrated in the fine engravings that decorate the Chief Engineer's memorial volume: *Del modo tenuto nel trasportare l'obelisco vaticano* . . . (Rome, 1589). But Domenico Fontana does not mention the artist of the inscriptions. Even the twentieth-century writer, J. A. F. Orbaan, who was an accomplished researcher in the Roman archives and had great respect for the inscriptions of Sixtus V, and knew of the existence of an album of Horfei's inscriptions, abstains from mentioning their creator. Yet it is a fact that the great masters who practised lettering in later generations follow the pattern which marked all the Sixtine inscriptions on monuments, including the great obelisk. What then do we know of their designer?

The primary document is in the Vatican Library (Vat. Lat. 5541).

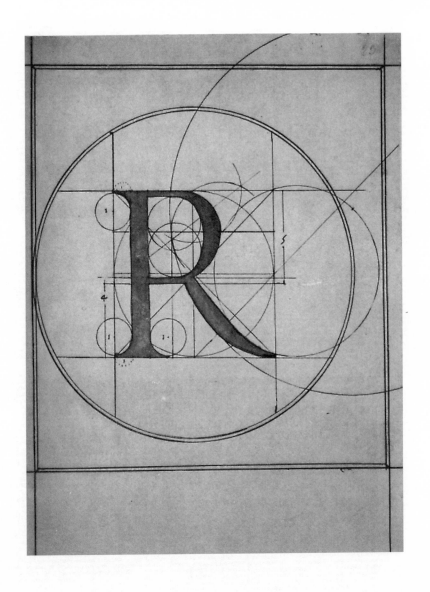

Giovambattiſta Palatino: design (reduced) for the conſtruction of an inscriptional capital (c. 1550?) Kunſtmuseum, Berlin

SIXTVS · V · PONT

AQVAM EX AGR

VIA PRAENEST ·

MVLTARVM COLL

DVCTV SINVOSO ·

MIL · XX · A CAPIT

FELICEMQ · DE NOM

```
M A X · P I C E N V S
   C O L V M N A E
N I S T R O R S V M
⊐ T I O N E  V E N A R
R E C E P T A C V L O
X X I I · A D D V X I T
N T E  P O N T  D I X I T
```

Luca Horfei, Varie Inscrittioni *(Rome, 1589): design for the inscription on the Fontana dell'Acqua Felice in Rome. Reduced*

Inscription on the Fontana dell'Acqua Felice in Rome as it was actually cut (photograph by Alinari)

Inscription on the south side of the Vatican obelisk
(photograph by James Mosley)

This manuscript was rediscovered by Signora Marzoli while preparing the catalogue for which the present essay was written. In her prefatory note, Signora Marzoli recorded that after many days of research in the Vatican Library, she found in a cased catalogue, more or less out of use, the card mentioning a manuscript of Horfei. Unfortunately the manuscript turned out to be in very poor condition. It was written on paper, and was evidently a 'fair copy' that the writer would use for a transcript upon vellum for presentation to the Pope. Search has not so far revealed the presentation copy, but the fair copy suffices for historical reasons since it contains the dedication to Sixtus V. Here, the artist, Luca Horfei (Lucas Orfeus Fanensis), describes himself as a scribe in the Apostolic Palace (Palatii Apostolici Scriptor). Horfei proudly says that the act of raising the obelisk as 'an eternal trophy of the Christian religion' was perfected by the decision to have the inscriptions cut by an 'artifex' capable of rendering with beauty every single letter or character (singulos letteras seu caractheres). Horfei then proceeds to say that he, who had devoted almost his entire life to the study of the capital letters (litterae maiores) commonly called Majusculas (quas vulgo MAIVSCVLAS appellat), had undertaken to execute a set of capitals equal in beauty to those of ancients.

Horfei then boasts that through the grace of God, etc., he had succeeded where so many had failed; and having undertaken the task [of drafting the inscriptions] he had devoted to it so much energy and skill that the elegance and beauty of his letters was everywhere recognized. Hence, he says 'I have decided to transcribe four of the most famous inscriptions on the Obelisk and to dedicate them to Your Holiness together with the entire alphabet of these same capitals (ipsarum MAIVSCVULARVM) which I shall soon print and publish (typis imprimenda) in their entirety, and these, he gladly acknowledges, 'will be under the most happy protection of Your Holiness and to the advantage of all scholars . . .'. The four inscriptions which the artist specifies will be mentioned below.

It is apparent, therefore, that Horfei was prepared to claim maximum credit for the designs of the capitals shown in his manuscript. The printed edition which he promised duly appeared. It is a very rare book and its bibliography has not so far been attempted. The title of the Newberry Library copy runs:

ALFABETO | Delle Maiuscole | Antiche Rom: | Del Signor | LVCA HORFEI | DA FANO | *Opera molt'utile* | a' Scrittori, | Pittori, e Scultori | Nella quale | *Con ragione Geometrica* | *S'insegnano le misure di d[e]tte l[ette]re.* | *Si stampano in Roma all'insegna del Luppo in Parione.*

Undated. Oblong quarto, 24 leaves, A–Z; 23 letters.

The title page is undated, but it is reasonable to suppose that it may have appeared between 1586, when the Vatican obelisk was raised, and *c.* 1589, when Horfei's *Varie Inscrittioni* was published. The pages following present a geometrical inscriptional alphabet from A to Z in a hatched style which, it is regrettable to say, reaches only a mediocre standard. It fails to reflect either the delicacy or the boldness of the manuscript.

Horfei's claim to have contrived the design of these capitals may be admitted. It is in the highest degree unlikely that such a man would make such a claim in such a place at such a time, if it were bogus. We may assume that Horfei was entitled to what credit there may be for the design of these capitals.

What, then, is the point in these inscriptions and the capitals which comprise them? What is novel in their style and, in so far as there is anything new in them, why was novelty thought necessary?

Was the motive purely aesthetic? One needs to know something of the personal preferences of Sixtus V. The catalogue of his own library which we know to be written in his own hand, and other autographs of his, need to be examined. It is abundantly possible that Horfei was to some extent guided by instructions given him by authority. Is there any sign of the intervention, at some point, of authority?

It may be said with confidence that the lettering of the four inscriptions mentioned with particular pride by Horfei and exhibited in *De Charaĉterum* represents, so to say, a 'modernized' version of the antique capitals. They are ŝill Roman but without being any longer Imperial. In effeĉt, the Sixtine capitals are a Chriŝian revision of the capitals that were part of the insignia of Auguŝus, Trajan and the succeeding pre-Chriŝian Emperors. Was this revision merely one more aspeĉt of the Pope's grandiose plans for the modernization of the Eternal City? Paŝor salutes Sixtus V as 'il creatore della nuova Roma'. Do we need to look for any further explanation for the change in lettering? It meant that a new architeĉtural policy was being executed. Possibly this is all the change signifies. On the other hand, it might well be that, consiŝently with the invocation of the Holy Cross in the text of the four inscriptions and the placing of the large emblem at the obelisk's extreme top, the Sixtine departure from the proportions of the then admired letters on the Trajan column was deliberate, authoritative and Chriŝian.

The policy is comparable, in its symbolism, with Sixtus's renovation of the columns of Trajan and Marcus Aurelius, and his ereĉtion of ŝatues of St Peter and St Paul on their respeĉtive summits. It was charaĉteriŝic of this Pope's building enterprises to emphasize the conversion of Rome from paganism to Chriŝianity. This was not irrelevant or superfluous in an age whose cult of the antique art had degenerated into the praĉtice of antique morals.

It is evident that Horfei's effort pleased the Pope, since he later accepted the dedication of the *Varie Iscrittioni del Santis. S.N. Siŝo V* (Rome, 1589). The inscriptions 'dissegnate in Pietra, et dal medesimo [Luca Horfei da Fano] fatte intagliare in Rame', while antique in a certain general sense, have a charaĉter obviously different from those on the Trajan column which Sixtus 'converted' into a pedeŝal for his ŝatue of St Peter. While the *Inscrittioni* advertise Horfei's conspicuous part in the design of the capitals, it provides reproduĉtions (to be seen in the *De Charaĉterum* of 1586–7 and the *Inscrittioni* of 1589) of inscriptions by Cesare Moreggio, then, perhaps, as eŝeemed as Horfei. An example is the inscription over the door of the ancient University of Rome. A new building had been begun for it by Alexander VI (Rodrigo Borgia) 1492–1503. The inſtitution was renamed the Collegio della Sapienza under Clement VII (Giulio de' Medici) 1523–34. Sixtus V, a former professor at the Sapienza, rescued the College from debt, modernized part of the building and decorated it with Moreggio's text INITIVM SAPIENTIAE EST TIMOR DOMINI whose capitals, according to Horfei, having been cut seven inches high, were lined with gold laid on cauſtic.

Since these words were written, the subjeƈt of Horfei and his inscriptions has been much illuminated by Mr Mosley's essay 'Trajan Revived', referred to above. Mr Mosley has been able, in many cases, to compare the prints with the aƈtual inscriptions, between which he has noted some surprising discrepancies. If Horfei's role in the Sixtine reforms is somewhat less clear than it seemed, knowledge of the inscriptional letter in Rome in the sixteenth century has been materially increased by this valuable paper.

Horfei was maſter of a fine florid late 'cancellarescha' as modelled by Cresci; he praƈtised a good, large minuscule of the type that would have been approved by Ruano; also he developed an original formal 'italic' minuscule which contraſted effeƈtively with his cursive 'cancellarescha'. As scriptor to the Capella Apoſtolica which we know better as the Sixtine Chapel (created by Sixtus IV (Francesco della Rovere) 1472–84), Horfei praƈtised a fine music in both ancient and modern notation. It goes without saying that he could perform a good gothic 'rotunda'.

To conclude, his supreme achievement is the Chriſtian revision of the pre-Chriſtian Roman Capital. That Horfei invented the Sixtine capital script in his mere capacity as a scribe is hardly probable.

As a cleric and Vatican official he would naturally attend to the suggeſtions of his superiors. The dedications of the *De Charaƈterum* and the *Varie Iscrittioni* prove that Horfei held the confidence of the Pope. It has been pointed out (Ernſt Kantorowicz, *Laudes Regiae*, Berkeley, Calif., 1946, p. 229, n. 32) that Sixtus V engraved on his

VARIE INSCRITTIONI
DEL SANTISS·S·N·SISTO·V·
PONT·MAX·

DA LVCA HORFEI DA FANO
Scrittore diſſegnate in Pietra,et dal
medeſimo fatte intagliare in Rame,

PER MOSTRARE LA LETTERA
Antica Romana
In diuerſe grandezze & compartimenti

Con alcune canccllarescl̄ecorſiuc variate
et altic manicrc dj lcttcrc neceſſ·

Title page (reduced) of Luca Horfei, Varie Inscrittioni *showing two
obelisks at right and left, with the arms of Sixtus V above*

SIXTVS ·V

INITIVM S
E
TIMOR

ONT·MAX

PIENTIAE

T

DOMINI

From *Luca Horfei,* Varie Inscrittioni:
'*The fear of the Lord is the beginning of wisdom.*' *Inscription for the*
doorway of the Collegio della Sapienza (which no longer survives in situ)

CHRISTVS VINCIT
CHRISTVS REGNAT
CHRISTVS IMPERAT
CHRISTVS
AB OMNI MALO
PLEBEM SVAM
DEFENDAT

P onente

From Luca Horfei (reduced), Varie Inscrittioni: *'Chriſt conquers, Chriſt reigns, Chriſt rules'*

coinage the Christian acclamation by which the Church superseded the
pre-Christian imperial and senatorial acclamation. Thus the *Christus
vincit* triad naturally became one of the four inscriptions to which Horfei referred with special pride in the dedication of *De Characterum* to
the Pope.

As Horfei gives it there is a fourth line to the original triad, so:
CHRITSVS VINCIT, CHRISTVS REGNAT, CHRISTVS IMPERAT.
To this text Horfei added the line: CHRITSVS AB OMNI MALO
PLEBEM SVAM DEFENDAT.

Horfei's other three texts are in harmony with the *Christus vincit*
triad. It seems to follow therefore, that the capitals should also be in
harmony with the texts. This would not be so if the Imperial model
were retained. Hence, Horfei's capitals must be acknowledged as having broken with the style that had been standard for a century and a
quarter, i.e. since the Imperial style had been revived by Donatello,
Mantegna, Feliciano, Matteo de' Pasti and Leon Battista Alberti. That
the capitals of the inscription conspicuously departed from the Imperial pattern is self-evident. It is difficult to believe that this change had a
purely aesthetic motive, for the new model was standardized for use on
all the Sixtine edifices, and also for the title page of the new text of the
Vulgate Bible (Rome, 1590). The capitals, therefore, must have been
backed by authority from the date of the raising of the Vatican obelisk
in 1586–7. It may reasonably be concluded, therefore, that the departure from the pre-Christian pattern is to be judged less as an aesthetic
aspect of Sixtus V's architectural activities than as one more dogmatic
affirmation of the Pope's determination to eradicate from Rome all
revived paganism. As may be verified from books in the present
collection the great writers who succeeded Horfei accommodated
themselves to the standard which he was the first to set in print.

We may now drop the subject. The foregoing paragraphs have concentrated upon the history and development of the chancery cursive writing and the roman capital lettering in Italy as illustrated by the volumes

liſted in the present Catalogue. Enough has been said, incidentally, to indicate that the colleƈtion here under consideration is not limited to these two scripts or to their career in sixteenth- and seventeenth-century Italy. The colleƈtion, indeed, does this, but its intereſt extends to later periods and other European countries.

The *raison d'être* of the successive changes in the form of weſtern script throughout the ages, from the ancient papyrus to the medieval vellum period and the modern use of paper as a medium, is clear and conſtant. The two main divisions into which weſtern script falls have already been mentioned, i.e. writing and lettering. The latter is ceremonial and as such is rightly expensive of time in its produƈtion and of material in its medium.

The former is utilitarian and as such rightly endeavours to be expeditious in its produƈtion and inexpensive in its medium. Any increase in demand for writing is equivalent to a demand for increase in speed of execution. Hence the general hiſtory of weſtern handwriting as diſtinƈt from lettering involves the syſtematic observation and critical appreciation of the effeƈt of the faƈtor of acceleration upon the shaping of individual letters, their ligaturing, grouping into words and spacing into sentences, etc. To assiſt this process, recourse was made to the aeſthetic faƈtor and it was by this means that hands that were originally little better than a hardly legible scribble were elevated into respeƈtability, and given a new career which was, on occasion, consecrated by religious and/or political faƈtors. On the whole the economic faƈtor was dominant. The interaƈtion of the aeſthetic faƈtor may be observed in the earlier and later specimens here liſted.

It only remains to lay emphasis upon the faƈt that, as the bookseller says in the Preface, additions, correƈtions, indications and locations of editions and copies are invited. The reason for making this appeal is manifeſt. These paragraphs have noted the contributions made to the Bibliography of Writing-Books. The attentive reader will have observed that the scientific ſtudy of the subjeƈt is by no means advanced. It is lamentable, for example, that nothing has been done towards a

Bibliography of the French Writing-Books since, many years ago, Jean Grand-Carteret (whom I gratefully remember and thank for the kind reception he gave me) printed a liſt of titles. The significance of the French school of calligraphers and engravers, and its influence in opening the way for an entirely new theoretical approach to letter-design in relation to typography has been emphasized by M. André Jammes, the learned bookseller in Paris, in his work *La Réforme de la Typographie Royale sous Louis XIV* (Paris, 1961). His researches in the Archives Nationales led to the discovery of the documents on the origins of the inquiry which resulted in the creation of the 'Romain du Roi' for the Imprimerie Royale.

It will then be seen that the 'baſtarde' in Alais's *L'Art d'écrire* (Paris, 1680) was considered by no less a figure than the Abbé Bignon as affording the beſt inspiration for the italic. This is high praise for the book (the copy in this colleƈtion is handsomely autographed by Paillasson) and for the author of the maxim 'La belle Ecriture demande un esprit gay pour son execution' (p. 9). He quickly adds 'Tous les violens et les débauches, abrutissent la subtilité de l'imagination, engourdissent le mouvement des doigts, et débilitent leur aƈtion'.

There is ſtill wanting a ſtudy of the Netherlandish Books. It is hoped that the circulation of this Catalogue may attraƈt ſtudents to a task, the discharge of which is essential, if we are to answer exaƈtly the queſtion why we write the way we do.

[*Written in 1961 and firſt printed in 1962*]

A NOTE ON THE TYPE

This book is set in the digital version of Monotype Fournier. It is one of a pair of faces, Monotype Fournier and Monotype Barbou, cut side by side in 1925–26, based on a single model. Both were attempts to recreate a type cut in Paris in the 1740s by Pierre Simon Fournier. Stanley Morison, then Typographical Advisor to the Monotype Corporation, preferred Barbou, which was slightly darker and had a blander, more even italic. Morison was overruled, and Fournier was the version commercially released. Some years later, Barbou was also cut in several sizes but was very seldom used. With every change of medium, the contest starts afresh. Digital Fournier might, in fact, be better – or might please Morison more – than digital Barbou, but we cannot know for sure, because Morison is not here to ask, and digital Barbou does not exist.

Letter Forms was printed and bound by Thomson-Shore Inc., Dexter, Michigan. The paper – which is Glatfelter laid – was made at the Spring Grove Mill in Spring Grove, Pennsylvania. It is of archival quality and acid-free.